GURU, PSYCHOTHERAPIST, AND SELF

A Comparative Study
of the Guru-Disciple Relationship
and the Jungian Analytic Process

by Peter P. Coukoulis

Published by

DeVorss & Company
P.O. Box 550
Marina del Rey, California 90291

10-85

Library of Congress Catalog Card No. 76-40851
ISBN: 0-87516-221-5 Paperback
ISBN: 0-87516-222-3 Hardback

Printed in the United States of America by
Book Graphics, Inc., California

TABLE OF CONTENTS

ACKNOWLEDGMENTS

This work first appeared as a doctoral dissertation and later was edited into its present form with the able assistance of Dr. Wesley Klein, and Eugene Jacobs, Librarian of the C.G. Jung Institute, Los Angeles.

I want to express my gratitude to the Nina Bushnell Foundation for its most valuable moral and financial support which made it possible for me to have a short visit at the C.G. Jung Institute and Clinic in Zurich, Switzerland, and to study extensively in India. Through these enhancing experiences I have been able to revise the dissertation and improve considerably the final draft of this study.

I wish to extend my appreciation to Dr. Haridas Chaudhuri for the guidance and assistance he gave me at various times in building the necessary scholastic background, providing constructive criticisms and evaluating phase by phase the entire body of this study.

I want to give my thanks to Dr. J. Marvin Spiegelman for his most meaningful criticisms regarding the psychological aspects of this investigation. His sustaining encouragement at the time was most valuable in completing the Jungian part of this comparative study.

Last but not the least, I wish to express my appreciation to my wife Beatrice, and my children Karen, Cynthia, Diane and Peter-Keith for their well-tried patience, cooperation and moral support which enabled me to persist and complete this undertaking.

Peter P. Coukoulis

GURU,

PSYCHOTHERAPIST

AND SELF

INTRODUCTION

Jung and investigators from other schools of psychotherapy have made significant contributions regarding the healing and personality transformation force that is active or dormant in the psychotherapist-patient relationship. Jung also examined the metaphysical-philosophical foundations of different Eastern movements, their religious practices and other attempts for attaining Self-realization. He evaluated some of these Eastern views and practices in the light of the empirical findings of modern psychology, including his own discoveries. As a result of these investigations, Jung pointed out that the West could learn much, psychologically, from the introverted wisdom of the East, provided that no attempts were made to imitate the Eastern ways.

During recent years, there has been increased interest in the investigation of the apparent and potential contributions of Eastern thought to Western psychotherapy. Little research, however, has been conducted regarding the psychological implications of the guru-disciple relationship in connection with the teachings and practices of Self-realization.

It is the purpose of this study (1) to examine the psychological aspects of the guru-disciple relationship in regard to Self-realization, as found in Eastern biographical and scriptural resources; (2) to make a comparative analysis of the guru-disciple relationship and the Jungian analyst-analysand relationship; and (3) to point out those elements in the

i

guru-disciple relationship which may have implications for a better understanding of the Jungian analytic relationship and of the Individuation Process.

By means of descriptive analysis, Eastern and Jungian concepts of the Self, its realization, its symbolic role and significance as a Supra-personal or Supreme Guru are presented and compared. Also various important facets of the Eastern guru-disciple, and the Jungian analyst-analysand relationship are discussed and psychologically evaluated.

Self-realization is the ultimate goal of the guru-disciple relationship. For this reason, a review is made of various Liberation and Self-realization concepts to ascertain whether or not basic similarities or differences exist among various Eastern systems, as well as the Western School of Analytical Psychology.

Most major schools accept the existence of a Universal Self, although there are several minor conceptual differences regarding its attributes and man's relationship to this Self. In some Buddhist and other schools, the existence of an Infinite Self is denied but an Ultimate or Transcendent Reality is either directly accepted or implied indirectly. Nearly all Eastern systems are basically in agreement that human existence and suffering are inseparable and that man's ultimate and uncompromising goal is Absolute Liberation, which can be attained by transcending the human condition.

The meaning and methods of transcending the human state of bondage vary widely. All schools, including Analytical Psychology, acknowledge the necessity for the ego to place itself into the service of the Ultimate Self or Reality and accept a subordinate, cooperative functional role. Some schools of thought emphasize the total extinction of the ego as part of the ultimate goal. Very few followers of any school, however, accept the total dissolution of the ego as an objective or a goal to be accomplished within the framework of their present human existence.

It could be stated that despite verbal-conceptual, cultural and methodological differences, the actual meaning and experiencing of the Self is the same in the Indian, Buddhist and Jungian systems.

In the following study, the role of the guru is discussed both in terms of its Supreme and human aspects.

The concept of the Supreme Guru is used synonymously with the concept of the Supreme or Transcendent Self, particularly when its wisdom and guiding attributes are stressed. The Eastern view of the Self or Supreme Guru corresponds in many ways to the formulation in Analytical Psychology of the Collective Unconscious. To establish an optimum relationship with the Supreme Guru, or the Jungian Unconscious, is man's basic goal in all major Eastern systems of spiritual attainment as well as in Analytical Psychology.

The human guru is broadly defined as a person whose profession or basic function is to assist his disciples in attaining Liberation or Self-realization. When the term is used in a higher sense, the guru is considered to be a person who has made partial or appreciable strides towards Self-realization before he attempts to assist others in establishing an intimate relationship with the Supreme Guru. Broadly speaking, the same personality attainment pre-requisites and goals apply to the Jungian analyst, although his methods and temporal objectives vary considerably.

The Eastern disciple whose objective is to make partial or appreciable progress in relation to his psychic development appears to follow a parallel path to that of the Jungian analysand. The main goal of the latter is likewise psychic development or Individuation, as well as coping with incidental life adjustment problems. Here, as in the case of comparing the guru with the analyst, the goal of the disciple and the analysand is the same but the methods and immediate objectives are in some ways different.

This study begins with the presentation and comparison of Eastern and Jungian concepts of the Self and its realization. More specifically, an examination is made of relevant conceptions found in the Upanishads, in some of the major Hindu schools of philosophy such as Vedānta, Nyāya, Sāṅkhya and Yoga, and in Buddhism. Basic similarities and minor existing differences among these systems are discussed briefly. Jung's concept of the Self and the Individuation process are discussed and compared with the Eastern views just mentioned.

Next, Tāntrik views regarding the suprapersonal aspects of the Guru are introduced. The qualifications and role of the human guru and disciple are discussed and compared with those of the Jungian analyst and analysand.

The symbolical nature of the guru-disciple relationship in the Bhagavad Gītā is then discussed in some detail. The psychological significance of the dialogue and kinship between Kṛṣṇa representing the Divine Self as Guru, and Arjuna, representing the ego-conscious man as the disciple, is examined. This is followed by a concise presentation of Sri Aurobindo's views on the guru and his relationship to the disciple. The attribute of the Divine as Guru is stressed in the latter. Aurobindo's concept of the Divine Birth with the mutual involvement and union between the Divine and man is also discussed, and the attitudes and approach of the human guru and the disciple are brought out and are compared to those of the Jungian analyst and analysand.

At this phase, the study turns to an examination of two specific gurus and their interaction with their disciples. Psychologically significant events in Sri Ramakrishna's life are presented. A psychological examination is made of Ramakrishna's experiences as a devotee. His various methods as a guru, and particularly his use of devotional practices, are discussed and compared to the techniques and over-all approach of the Jungian analyst. Finally, several aspects of the guru-disciple relationship described in the legendary biography of Milarepa, a great Tibetan Tāntrik Buddhist yogi, are examined from the standpoint of Analytical Psychology. The biography is viewed symbolically, and Milarepa's strivings and psychic development are evaluated psychologically as the 'journey of the hero.' The attitudes and commitment of the disciple, the outlook and methods of the guru, and the use of dreams for psychic guidance purposes, are examined and compared to the Jungian analytical situation.

Chapter I

EASTERN VIEWS AND JUNG'S VIEWS
ON SELF-REALIZATION

In the East, man's attempt to free and liberate himself from pain and suffering was most likely the greatest motivating element in the development of doctrines and practices of liberation and realization of the Self. Īsvarakṛṣna, the author of the earliest Sāṅkhya treatise, stated that the foundation stone of Sāṅkhya is man's desire to free himself from the torture of the three sufferings which are: (1) celestial misery provoked by the gods; (2) terrestrial misery caused by nature and (3) inner or organic misery.[1] Patañjali wrote, "All is suffering for the sage."[2] In various Buddhist writings plentiful references are found regarding human existence as nothing but pain and misery. This tremendous concern with relieving and releasing man from suffering was not restricted to the few well-known Eastern movements just mentioned. With a few exceptions, all major Eastern religious-philosophical systems shared and dealt with this concern in one way or other.

A review of pertinent concepts of the Self and of Self-realization was undertaken at this section of the study in order to facilitate the subsequent examination of the guru-disciple relationship.

1

Eastern Concepts of the Self and Its Realization

Radhakrishnan, in his introduction to *The Principal Upaniṣads,* explains that passing from the Vedic hymns to the Upaniṣads there is a shift from the objective to the subjective. From fascination with the outside world the focus is placed upon meditation on the significance of the Self. The Real at the heart of the universe is reflected in the infinite depths of the soul. It is the human Self that contains the clue to the interpretation of nature. The Upaniṣads give in some detail the path of the inward journey by which the individual souls get at the Ultimate Reality. Truth is within man and the different Vedic gods are envisaged subjectively. The Kausitaki Brāhmana is quoted as saying, 'He is, indeed, initiated whose gods within him are initiated, mind by mind, voice by voice.' The Vedic gods serve to mediate between pure thought and the intelligence of the dwellers in the world of senses.[3]

The word 'Brahman' is used in the Upaniṣads to indicate the Supreme reality. The derivation suggests to burst forth, gushing forth, bubbling over or ceaseless growth. It later came to be known as the creative principle, the cause of all existence. The word suggests a fundamental kinship between the aspiring spirit of man and the spirit of the universe which it seeks to attain.[4] Brahman, the first principle of the universe, is known through ātman, the innerself of man. The Satapatha Brāhmana and the Chāndogya Upaniṣad stated: 'Verily this whole world is Brahman' and also, 'This soul of mine within the heart, this is Brahman.' 'That person who is seen in the eye, He is ātman, that is Brahman.'[5]

Spirit or soul as a transcendent and autonomous principle has been accepted by most Indian philosophies with the exception of the Buddhists and the materialists. These various schools use different means by which they attempt to prove the existence and essence of the spirit. Nyaya considers soul-spirit as absolute, without qualities, unknowing. Vedānta defines the soul-self (ātman) as "being" or "consciousness". It regards spirit as universal and eternal reality, dramatically enmeshed in the temporal illusion of creation (māyā). Sāṅkhya and Yoga deny spirit (puruṣa) any attribute and relation. The knowledge of puruṣa is in the nature of pure Self-shining consciousness.

Buddha and many of his followers denied the outright existence of the Self. The continuity of a person from different childhood states, youth and old age, and from birth to birth is explained through means of the continuity of the stream of successive states that compose man's life. There is a causal connection in the continuity of man's life series. This stream of momentariness extends itself backwards and forwards and in that manner the past, present and future continuity in one's life is explained. The concept of the soul in this way is replaced by an unbroken stream of consciousness. The current state of consciousness inherits its traits causally from previous ones and by these means memory becomes comprehensible without introducing the concept of the soul.[6] The soul or self in Buddhism is an illusion as well as any conditioned mode of living. But this view applies only phenomenologically. A close examination of the teachings expounded by the major Mahā-yana schools indicates, however, that an Ultimate or Transcendent Reality is accepted in most cases, and where it is not directly accepted, it is implied indirectly.

Many writers have pointed out that the difference between the concept of ātman, as found in various Hindu movements, and that of Nirvāna, as expounded in Buddhism, is only apparent and not essential. Coomaraswami has commented on this matter with clarity and convincingly.[7] Dasgupta, while explaining the affinities between Vedānta and Mahāyāna Buddhism arrived at the same conclusion.[8]

In some systems like Sāṅkhya and Vedānta, ultimate liberation is attained by means of metaphysical knowledge. In others, like Yoga and Buddhism, liberation is possible only through experimental knowledge, which means practice that includes and requires action, and practice of asceticism. While the methods and the intensity of ascetic or disciplinary action vary, and in some cases radically, the effort is placed upon affecting and transforming directly the practitioner's psycho-physical experiential mode of living and being.

It has already been pointed out that certain conceptual differences exist among the various Eastern schools regarding the nature of the Self or Ultimate Reality. Despite these differences, there is an essential area of agreement. All presuppose that human existence and suffering are inseparable and that man's ultimate and uncompromising goal is absolute liberation. Freedom from bondage can be attained only by transcending the human condition, which necessitates surpassing the human personality. Such a goal, by Western standards, appears anti-social and pessimistic. By Eastern standards, however, there is optimism and idealistic morality in this approach. With a few exceptions, most of these systems are deeply concerned with the liberation of all humanity, and not infrequently there is genuine concern regarding the liberation of all living beings. This is particularly stressed and dramatized in Buddhism, and various post-Śankara Vedānta movements.[9]

The Eastern ideal of liberation goes beyond arbitrary notions to release man from human suffering. Among others, Eliade notes the initiatory character of liberation doctrines.[10] The student or practitioner, in his attempt to recover the initial non-duality or primordial situation, must separate himself from the human situation. As in an initiation, he must die to be reborn. His detachment or death from the human situation makes possible his return to the beginning primordial unity. But his new birth is not a repetition of a natural one; the candidate does not return to the profane world to which he has just died during his initiation; he finds a sacred world corresponding to a new mode of being inaccessible to the natural (profane) level of existence.[11] While referring to the initiatory aspects of yoga, one might conclude that in this conscious conquest of the freedom ideal, man, by liberating himself, creates the spiritual dimension of freedom and introduces it into the Cosmos and life.

The Self and Individuation in Analytical Psychology

Jung, like most Eastern schools, considers the Self as indescribable and only to be explained by means of symbols, which are, according to him, the best possible expressions of an unknown fact. The Self is the totality of all existence. Defining it psychologically, he says it is:

> . . . a union of conscious (masculine) and unconscious (feminine). It stands for the psychic totality. So

formulated it is a psychological concept. Empirically, however, the self appears spontaneously in the shape of specific symbols, and its totality is discernible above all in the mandala (symbol of unity, birthplace of the self) and its countless variants. Historically, these symbols are authenticated as God images.[1][2]

Jung also defines the Self as the archetype of wholeness.[1][3] In a sense, the Self can be characterized as a kind of compensation for the conflict between inside and outside because it has the character of a result of a goal attained. So the Self is our life's goal, for it is the most complete expression of that fateful combination we call individuality, the full flowering not only of the single individual, but of the group in which each adds his portion to the whole.[1][4]

The Self is further defined as:

> A quantity that is superordinate to the conscious ego. It embraces not only the conscious but also the unconscious psyche, and is therefore, so to speak, a personality which we also are.[1][5]

As a further implication to the definition just given, Esther Harding, on several occasions, refers to the Self as being the center and container of the psyche. She goes into lengthy explanation regarding the problems as well as the desirability for such a definition.[1][6] In the brief description of the Individuation process which follows, this concept of the Self will be more fully understood.

The main purpose of Self-realization, according to Analytical Psychology, is to shift the center of the personality from the ego to the Self. In this respect there is full agreement with the Eastern approach to Self-realization. To stress this point, Jung says:

> To experience and realize this self is the ultimate aim of Indian Yoga, and in considering the psychology of the self we would do well to have recourse to the treasures of Indian wisdom. In India, as with us, the experience of the self has nothing to do with intellectualism; it is a vital happening which brings about a

fundamental transformation of personality. I have called the process that leads to this experience the 'process of individuation.'[17]

Jung also recommends the study of alchemy, particularly for psychologists. Alchemy, in its attempt to reconcile the opposites, with its preoccupation to transform the grosser elements into finer ones, whether it be in physical nature or in the psyche, has developed a rich symbolism that is greatly helpful to us in understanding the Individuation process.

The Individuation process is started off when one begins to become conscious of the shadow, a negative personality component, which is made up of everything that will not fit in, and adapt to, the laws and regulations of conscious life.[18] The integration or humanization of the Self starts from the conscious side. Its purpose is to make us aware of our selfish aims. It is an act of recollection, a gathering together of what is scattered, of things in us that are not properly related, and coming to terms with ourselves in an endeavor to achieve full consciousness. Individuation appears, on the one hand, as the synthesis of a new unity which previously consisted of scattered particles, and on the other hand, as the revelation of something which existed before the ego and is, in fact, its creator and totality.[19]

Unconscious becoming or unconscious Individuation is hardly a concern for Analytical Psychology. Its main challenge, contribution and function is to understand and facilitate conscious realization of oneself with the resulting increase in consciousness. Here consciousness must confront the unconscious and a balance between the opposites must be found. One must depend on symbols which make the irrational union of opposites possible. They are produced spontaneously by the unconscious and are amplified by the conscious. The central symbols of the process describe the Self which is realized by the union of the opposites, a union made possible by these symbols.[20]

Harding summarizes the meaning of Individuation by describing it as the process by which the individual progresses towards completeness within himself and becomes truly a man.[21]

Analytical Psychology is concerned with the empirical examination of the Self as it pertains to man as a whole, while at the same time keeping fully aware that it is dealing predominantly with men greatly influenced by their Western psychic and cultural heritage. The Eastern schools are dealing with the same Self as it essentially pertains to the fullness and wholeness of man. The philosophical, metaphysical-introspective influence of the Eastern mind and culture has had a considerable impact on the formulations and practices regarding Self-realization. It seems reasonable to say that although conceptual differences exist among various Eastern schools and Analytical Psychology regarding the Self and its realization, such differences are minor. Essentially the meaning and experiencing of the Self is the same in the Indian, Buddhist, and Jungian systems despite differences in technique, verbal-conceptualization, and cultural factors.

Chapter II

TĀNTRIK VIEWS REGARDING
THE GURU-DISCIPLE RELATIONSHIP

In the East, it was traditionally helpful and, in most cases, necessary for a seeker attempting to attain Self-realization to have a spiritual guide or preceptor called a guru. The novice assumed the role of a disciple and was usually known as a śiṣya.

A guru may be one who has no spiritual attainment, but ordained as a priest or in some other frequently inherited capacity, has been invested with the right to give initiation and upadeśa (spiritual instruction-training). A guru may also be one who has partial but not deep and thorough attainment. To that extent, he may give a somewhat more potent upadeśa than the guru who has made no spiritual strides. In the highest sense, however, the role of the guru as a spiritual preceptor has been a most challenging one. He is not merely a teacher concerned with imparting religious instruction verbally and/or performing special rites. Generally speaking, he is entrusted to oversee the full spiritual development of his śiṣyas and guide them through the arduous process of Self-realization. This is possible only if the guru himself has established a relationship with the Wholeness of the Self. It thus becomes apparent that an investigation of the human guru-disciple relationship must take into consideration the separate and joint relationship of these two with the wisdom of the Self.

8

A superficial examination of Tāntrik views on the guru-disciple relationship may give the impression that mainly traditional superstitious practices are involved here. A more careful evaluation, however, will show that much can be gained if such views and practices are not examined literally but psychologically for their rich symbolic and intuitive insight. Keeping this in mind, pertinent aspects of the guru-disciple relationship will be brought out and discussed in this chapter.

The Supra-Personal Attributes of the Guru

Among the many qualities ascribed to Ultimate Reality, that of the Supreme Guru is used to designate the universal inspiring and guiding force that manifests itself in various personal forms to enable the human seeker to attain liberation. In a broad sense the word "guru" represents the directing concern and involvement of a supra-personal intelligence in the process of Self-realization at the human plane.

In various Tāntrik writings reference is made to the transpersonal or universal attributes of the guru. On some occasions the Supreme Guru is equated to Brahman as found in the most frequently defined expressions of this concept. On other occasions, however, certain qualities that describe the process, or some of the necessary elements that go into the process, are used as synonyms for the Supreme Guru concept. A typical illustration of this point is found in the Guptasādhana Tantra where it is said:

> Guru is Brahmanā. Guru is Vishnu. Guru is Mahaś-vara Himself. Guru is the place of pilgrimage. Guru is the sacrifice. Guru is charity (that is the religious merit acquired by means of charity). Guru is devotion and austerities. Guru is Surya (sun). The entire Universe is Guru.[1]

According to several writings nothing surpasses in significance the aspect of the Ultimate expressed as Guru. In the Guptasādhana even Śāstra (scriptures), Mantra, or the fruit of religious rites are not greater than Guru, nor is even Śiva greater than Guru. No form or appearance is superior to that of Guru —

that is to say, by performance of Sādhana of Guru alone one becomes Siddha in all the other modes of Sādhana.[2]

The Rudrayāmala asserts that no worship or devotion can be properly motivated if it ignores its relationship and allegiance to the Guru ideal and practices. It dramatically states:

> By devotion to Guru a Jīva (religious seeker) will attain the state of Indra (Lord of the Celestials), but by devotion to Me he will become swine. (That is to say, if a Jīva whilst giving devotion to his Iṣṭadevatā, yet slights his Guru, he becomes swine.) In fact, no Śāstra speaks of anything which is superior to devotion to the Guru.[3]

In the Tantras as well as in the Upaniṣads and other Eastern scriptures there is no clear cut dichotomy between the Supreme Guru and the human guru. Here the word 'Guru' exists to point out the supra-personal qualities of the concept and its meaningful application to the searching temporal man. The human guru is most important but only because he ideally or in lesser degree symbolizes the guiding wisdom of the Self. As a concrete living person of deeper insights and spiritual attainment, the human guru becomes the natural symbol and, figuratively speaking, the actual embodiment of the Supreme Guru. Under such circumstances the guru-disciple relationship assumes a profound significance. The śiṣya is prepared or at least prepares himself to treat his guru with utmost respect, trust and devotion. He is willing to undergo many hardships in carrying out the instructions and commands of his guru. The religious traditions of his culture assist him considerably to develop such attitudes and outlook.

The uniqueness and importance ascribed to the Supreme Guru, and how he is symbolically manifested and experienced through the human guru enhancing, therefore, the role of the latter, is well described in the following quotation taken from the Tantra Tattva:

> Although Gurus have different physical bodies, they are embodiments of the One. Śāstra has, therefore, said: 'He who is my Guru is the Guru of the world.'[4]

Despite occasional extremism and the emphasis placed at times on a popular level of understanding and appeal, Tāntrism stresses the forms and personifications of the Supreme Guru in a way that does not conflict or detract from the concept of the Guru as a Supreme Principle or Impersonal Universal Self. On the contrary, in many Tantras the impersonal, universal aspects of the Supreme Guru are either implied or more directly declared as such. Furthermore, Sir John Woodroffe in his introduction to the *Tantra Tattva (Principles of Tantra)* reminds us of evidence regarding the antiquity of the Tantras. He states that the Tantras were introduced and accepted side by side along with other Hindu scriptures; that very often there were similarities between basic ideas and recommended practices found in many of the Upaniṣads and those found in the Tantras; and behind the apparent dualism of Tāntrism there were only differences of method and no basic conflicts when compared with the impersonal non-dualism of Vedānta.[5]

The Qualifications of the Human Guru and Disciple

In many scriptural writings it has been repeatedly emphasized that only to the extent that one has penetrated the depths of his own nature and has experienced its ultimate uniqueness, to that extent he may also be able to guide others toward reaching this goal. It is in this sense that a guru is expected to have attained liberation or enlightenment before he attempts to guide others. This point is well explained by both Sri Aurobindo and Sri Ramakrishna in later chapters of the study. The Kulāgama offers a good illustration on this matter. It states:

> Those who are instructed by sages possessed of spiritual knowledge become undoubtedly possessed of spiritual knowledge themselves . . . For though a learned man can save an ignorant man, the latter can never save another ignorant man. A boat can carry a stone across the river, but a stone can never carry another stone across it. One person can never guide another person along a path which he has never trod himself; but he who has travelled along any one path, reached its end, and thus known the goal of all paths, can, standing at the

centre to which all paths tread, call to the travellers on each of the paths, and thus help them to reach the place where he himself stands.[6]

In Tāntrik writings in addition to spiritual qualifications of the guru, there can also be found social and physical ones. These may be considered in some ways as arbitrary and restrictive, and in other ways as providing constructive guidelines in accordance with religious and cultural traditions. The Rudrayāmala spells out some of the conditions under which a woman may become a guru. In regard to this matter it says:

> She must be a Kulīna (practicing Kulācāra, Kulajā, born of a Kaula or respectable family) of auspicious appearance, fair face (literally, 'whose face is like the moon') and lotus-eyed; decked with gold and gems; endowed with intellect, calmness of mind, and all good qualities; a follower of her Acarā (practice that a particular person should follow), good, pious, and chaste, with control over her senses; of good conduct and devoted to the service of her elders; proficient in Mantras and in their meaning; ever engaged in Japa (recitation of Mantra) and devoted to the worship of her Iṣtadevatā (one's own chosen Deity). . .[7]

The Rudrayāmala continues with many more detailed requirements regarding the qualifications of a woman guru and also stating certain restrictions for widows who wish to become gurus.

In several Tantras, restrictions of caste play a significant role in determining the qualifications of a guru. As a general rule, a member of a higher caste, if otherwise qualified, is permitted to be a guru to members of his own caste and to those of lower ones. Members of a lower caste may not be gurus to members of a higher caste.[8]

Many of the Tantras and some of the Purāṇas stress the role of the 'guru family.' According to these, the right to be a guru for initiation and religious instructional purposes is inherited and passed on at the family level from generation to generation. Birth into a guru family, however, does not automatically authorize one to be a guru unless such a person meets all other prescribed qualifications.[9]

The Rudrayāmala and the Kalpacintāmani alert the disciple to abandon a guru of low moral character or one who has a physical defect or poor health such as severe chronic illness.[10] The author of the *Tantra Tattva* elaborates on this issue as follows:

> ... if after a person has been initiated his Guru contracts any of the above-mentioned faults, he should continue to honour and not abandon him; but one who has previous to such initiation contracted any of these faults should never be made a Guru.[11]

Many of the caste, sex, health and moral integrity requirements that apply to the guru also apply to the disciple. The śiṣya has come to the guru because of his spiritual ignorance, but his attitude must be one of highest devotion and respect to his guru. The human guru represents the Supreme Guru. Only a most serious and consistent attitude of treating the human guru as a genuine embodiment of the Supreme Guru will create, according to Tāntrik teachings, the right conditions for spiritual revelation and attainment. The author of the *Tantra Tattva,* in order to illustrate how essential is devotion to the guru, quotes the scriptures in which Bhagavān (a personification of the Supreme God) incarnated as a devotee and took as a guru his very own special disciple, Nārada. Then He, Bhagavān, practiced to Himself the yoga of meditation while still living in the womb waiting to be born.[12]

This scriptural incident also deals with the concept of Avatarhood, which will be discussed later in the chapter of the study by the title, "The Guru-Disciple Relationship in the Bhagavad Gītā." In any event, this illustration serves to dramatize the strong conviction found among the Tāntriks that a conscious human being needs to accept another conscious human being as his guru, instead of accepting an inanimate object or an abstract idea as his guru, or studying the scriptures or meditating without a guru. If Bhagavan found it literally or symbolically necessary to accept a guru to practice the yoga of meditation when he was incarnated, it is even more imperative, according to this view, that human beings accept a human guru.

The Gautamīya Tantra lists several of the characteristics which a śiṣya should possess:

> Born in a noble family; of pure spirit; seeking that which is the necessity of Puruṣa (Puruṣārtha — the four-fold object of Dharma, Artha, Kāma, and Moksa); learned in the Vedas; wise; devoted to the service of parents; knower of Dharma — religion, duty, etc. — and a doer thereof; attached to the personal service of Guru; proficient in Śāstra — scriptures —; strong of body and mind; ever desirous of doing good to Jivas; a doer of acts which bear good fruit in the next world; devoted to the service of Guru in speech, mind, body, and with his wealth; mindful only of acts the fruit of which endure; with control over the senses; free from sloth; free from delusion and vanity; devoted to Guru's son, wife, and so forth, as to the Guru himself — of such qualities should a śiṣya be possessed, otherwise he is but a source of trouble for his Guru.[13]

It can be seen here that the disciple not only is expected to have helpful and constructive attitudes but he is expected to have a considerable amount of spiritual attainment. Concern was ever expressed to avoid having the śiṣya be a source of trouble for his guru. One may wonder, if the disciple already possesses such qualities what is left for the guru to do and what is the disciple doing there in the first place? One of the probable answers is that partial attainment is expected on the part of the disciple. Another possible answer may be that the positive qualities of the disciple are dramatized or used in a relative fashion. It should be remembered that many of the Tantras were written for the benefit of non-intellectual lay people over a long period of time and literal interpretation in many cases would present insurmountable difficulties. What is consistently stressed in most Tantras, regardless of other verbal excesses, is that the human guru should carefully test his prospective disciple, and the disciple should test his guru to find out first hand if each is taking his role seriously and is worthy of his chosen profession.[14]

The Qualifications and Outlook of the
Jungian Analyst and Analysand

A review of the Jungian qualifications and a comparison of these with those of the Tāntrik guru and disciple disclosed both differences and similarities.

The would-be analyst must undertake extensive training over a period of several years before he is even admitted into an analyst training program. He must be either a licensed physician, or a recognized psychologist; or in lieu of these, in some instances, he is permitted to complete an advanced graduate school training course in the humanities or in an allied area. As a prerequisite or at least a corequisite to analytical training, the candidate must undergo a personal analysis which is financially expensive and quite demanding in terms of personal involvement. Once he is accepted in the training program, he must devote at least three or four years to intensive training involving: (1) further personal analysis; (2) conducting analysis under supervision; and (3) developing a theoretical framework which is necessary to supplement his analytical and clinical psychic growth experiences.[15]

It can be noticed that the preparation and over-all training of a Jungian analyst is a lengthy, extensive and demanding endeavor. There are, however, no rigid physical or hereditary-caste restrictions such as those mentioned earlier, applicable to the Tāntrik guru. Nevertheless, in the case of a Jungian analyst, there are serious intellectual and in some cases socio-economic restrictive requirements. A person who does not have the intellectual aptitude to complete rigid academic requirements will not be allowed to become an analyst. In many countries and in sub-cultures of others, persons who might have the capacity, interest and all other necessary qualities for completing an analyst training program would never have such an opportunity due to socio-economic restrictions.

Referring to moral qualifications, Jungian analyst trainees are screened on the basis of their capacity for individuation. In this respect, personal integrity traits and responsible dealing with collective relationships and needs are taken into consideration. There are not, however, any particular sets of moral rules or standards that analysts or trainees must follow, other than those affecting any citizen in his private life or occupation. The professional code of ethics applicable to psychotherapists in general, in a sense, would provide some minimum moral conduct guidelines for an analyst to follow.

It should be remembered that there are two basic types of analytic patients: (1) those who come to analysis because of life adjustment difficulties wishing to be cured of their mental suffering and problems; and (2) those who are trying to make strides towards Individuation. The latter ones may have originally come to analysis to be cured of a neurosis or some other mental ailment and later, as they began to progress, they decided to concentrate on individuation, in addition to dealing with their adjustment problems. In either case, the analysand is not expected to live in his analyst's home and serve him and his family with utmost respect and devotion. The patient is usually required to attend promptly the scheduled analytic sessions and pay the agreed fee which in many cases is considered to be high. The analytic relationship may terminate at any time if either the patient or the analyst or both decide to do so.

There are no basic moral demands made upon the patient. Often, however, during the healing of a neurosis or some other disturbance, there is a minor or major shift in the analysand's moral values and outlook.

Patients whose main objective is Individuation enter the analytic situation with a sense of great commitment and responsibility. In addition to meeting such secondary requirements as fees and attending the analytic sessions regularly, they also often devote a few or even several hours weekly dealing with their unconscious fantasy and dream contents. In various ways they try to assimilate unconscious elements and expand their consciousness. Such an undertaking sooner or later must, to a great extent, be tackled outside the analyst's office despite the tremendous value of the analyst-analysand person-to-person relationship.

Fordham stated that Individuation presupposes that the problem is not one of developing the ego but of differentiating it from and bringing it into relation with the unconscious, out of which the Self appears as an experience apart from the ego.

In this regard the transference can be more obscure and less intense, more transpersonal, yet the analyst's reactions are essential.[16] It seems as if Fordham is stressing the qualitative aspects of the analyst-analysand relationship. While the quantitative factors cannot be ignored, they are of lesser importance. In this respect Jung and other analysts would agree, although they might have different approaches in dealing with the qualitative elements of the analytic relationship.

It should be added that at times non-individuation patients may assume a great personal responsibility for the outcome of their analytical work. With encouragement and guidance received through the analytic relationship, they may start in daily life to relate unconscious contents to their conscious situation. The scope, depth and length of such an undertaking varies considerably from patient to patient.

It was indicated earlier that much Tāntrik literature deals with great personality, moral, cultural and physical demands in regard to the qualifications of gurus and disciples. Some of these qualifications can be interpreted in a broad and liberal sense, while others are specifically spelled out in rigid and restrictive terms. The major intent for having high qualifications has been the recognition that spiritual attainment demands a most dedicated attitude and arduous and rigorous preparation. The author of the *Tantra Tattva* repeatedly has expressed grave concern regarding the general Hindu neglect and adulteration of guru-disciple practices.[17] He refers particularly to recent times, but this problem has existed from the very inception of Tāntrism.

Essentially only relatively few gurus and śiṣyas have been able to meet the traditional high qualification standards. In that sense, there is a parallel between the Western Jungian analysand and the Tāntrik devotee. In another sense, there is a distinct difference between the individuation type of analysand and the rare Tāntrik disciple. The first is prepared to put forth much effort within the challenging yet familiar socio-physical background of living. The latter is prepared for a more radical commitment that may constantly shake every phase of his socio-physical existence. Jung stated that Zen monks are ready to make any sacrifice for the sake of the truth but very often psychotherapy deals with the most stubborn of Europeans.[18] Jung has stated, on other occasions, that various Eastern seekers, and that would include the Tāntriks, are committed and culturally suited for a more radical approach to Self-realization.

The Tāntriks have understood that various kinds of human relationships and particularly special phases of a one-to-one relationship are essential to dissolve misconceptions about one's own limited personality outlook and to develop a deeper and broader understanding of one's own being. Psychologists would say that properly motivated intimate relationships of an intense nature facilitate the dissolution of projections and promote a more integrated outlook. By 'properly motivated' only certain types of relationships, including the analytical, would be implied. Openness to experience would be a major criterion in deciding which relationships are conducive to personality growth.

The human guru-disciple relationship under favorable conditions attempts to deal with the dissolution of the parental images when examined from the viewpoint of Analytical Psychology.[19] The main objective is not to fixate the disciple's attention and devotion on the personal-ego aspects of the human guru. The main goal is to activate the archetypal forces dealing with the transpersonal aspects of the guru. Through the human aspects of the relationship an attempt is made to react to and differentiate between the personal projected contents and the essential nature of one's experiencing, and, dealing with projections, initiate integration and continue with the Self-realization process.

In later chapters of the study, concerning Sri Ramakrishna and Milarepa, more detailed aspects of the Tāntrik guru-disciple relationship are introduced and examined.

Chapter III

THE GURU-DISCIPLE RELATIONSHIP
IN THE BHAGAVAD GĪTĀ

All Indian authorities agree that the Gītā is the essence of all sacred writings. Śaṅkarācharya, in the beginning of his commentary, calls the Gītā "the collected essence of all the Vedas."[1] In this work Kṛṣṇa, as a personification of God, an Avatār, is involved in a most significant dialogue with his chosen disciple, the warrior Arjuna. According to Aurobindo, there are three things in the Bhagavad Gītā that are essential in relation to spiritual realization. These are almost symbolic, typical of the most profound relations and problems of the spiritual life and of human existence at its roots. They are the Divine personality of the Teacher, his characteristic relations with his disciple, and the occasion of his teachings.[2] Regarding the first, the significance of the Divine Teacher's personality was discussed earlier. Any further pertinent ideas in this area and the last two, the Teacher's relations with his disciple and the occasion of his teachings, will be examined in this chapter.

Preliminary Aspects of the Relationship

Although the Gītā accepts the human Avatarhood which serves an important function, it is its concept of the Eternal Avatār, the God in man always present in the human being who

19

manifested in a visible form and speaks to the human soul, that illumines the meaning of life and the secret of divine action and knowledge. Krsna is not presented as the hero of the battlefield, but is standing behind the great action of the Mahābhārata as if he were symbolically its hidden centre and guide. He appears as the charioteer friend and teacher of the warrior, Arjuna. The chosen disciple, however, is not aware of the Divine nature of the Guru. Ordinarily, the human soul is only potentially the eternal companion of the Divine. It needs to be awakened to this companionship and to begin, as the Gītā would say, to live in God.[3]

The awakening to the Divine kinship does not occur to Arjuna until a later stage. Even after Krsna's initial revelation of his Divine nature, Arjuna soon forgot that his Guru and companion was God, the Lord himself. It is only much later through the implied insights obtained during the persisting dialogue between the finite disciple and the apparently human but essentially Divine Guru that Arjuna gained a realization of the Lord's true nature.

Although there are strong indications that a historical Krsna did exist, what concerns us here is the impact of the role played by Krsna, the Avatār of the epic in relation to his morally confused and bewildered disciple. Aurobindo sees Arjuna as representing man in a world-struggle and divinely guided movement of man and nations; he (Arjuna) typifies in the Gītā the human soul of action brought face to face through that action in its highest and most violent crisis with the problem of human life and its incompatibility with the spiritual state or even with a purely ethical ideal of perfection.[4] Arjuna, the Ksatriya from the warrior class, knew his duty and was not afraid to fight. Only when he reflected upon the destructive moral-social consequences of such action, did he refuse to fight and placed himself in an unresolved conflict. Being in such a terrible moral and spiritual crisis, he desperately began to search for a solution.

It is at this point in the Gītā that the guru-disciple relationship is initiated. Psychologically the classical saying, "When the disciple is ready the Master or Guru appears" applies here. The Guru appears in the guise of the Charioteer-friend, and Arjuna asks him for help, to give him the answer to his predicament. The Gītā describes this relationship poetically in the nature of a prolonged dialogue in the midst of the battlefield which represents the irreconcilable conflicts of the mundane world of action. The dialogue represents the three stages through which action rises out of the human into the Divine plane leaving the bondage of the lower for the freedom of the higher. In the first stage, by renunciation of desire, man the doer, performs works as sacrifice to a deity who is the Supreme Self, although not yet realizable by him in his own being; in the second stage, both the claim of being the doer of action and the desire for the fruit of action must be renounced in the knowledge and realization of the Self as the equal, inactive and immutable principle of all works, as the operation of Universal force, of the Nature-Soul (Prakriti), the unequal, active, mutable power; and in the third or last stage, the Supreme Self is seen governing Prakriti of whom the Soul in nature is a partial manifestation, by whom all works are directed in a complete transcendence through nature. To him love and adoration and the sacrifice of works have to be offered.

The primary significance of the dialogue and relationship between Kṛṣṇa and Arjuna lies in the interaction between the finite ego-centered seeker and the Supreme Guru. The role played by the human embodiment of the Guru is also helpful to understand the overall aspects of the relationship.

The Relationship of the Ego to the Self

Arjuna is not shown here as a devotee seeking spiritual attainment. He specifically asks Kṛṣṇa for a true law, a clear rule of action, a path by which he can again confidently walk. He does not ask for the secret or meaning of life, he only asks for a dharma, a set of standards or rules for his conduct. But the Guru is not prepared to offer and will not give the disciple any outward rules of action. He intends to lead him into the higher life and help him give up all dharmas except the one broad and vast rule of living consciously in the Divine and acting from that consciousness.[5]

Krsna's immediate reply to the disciple's plea for help and guidance was the pointing out of the difficulty which arises by confusing action with the desire and results of action. He later says (Ch. II: 47), "Thy right is only to action; let thy right be never to the result; nor may thou be the cause of the result of action, nor may there be in thee attachment to inaction." In another section (Ch. III: 8, 9, 15 & 19) the Guru urges the disciple to perform his proper action for action is superior to inaction; not even the bodily functions and voyage can be accomplished by inaction. Only actions performed for God's sake do not bind or limit. The all-pervading spirit is ever established in action. A man performing action without attachment attains to the Supreme.

The Guru here, dealing with a disciple who like most men is engrossed in the world of activity, attempts to elucidate the deeper meaning of action. His role and mission is not to assist with solving temporal problems of life in the mundane world, although that may at times be a secondary incidental function of even a great guru. Krsna, the embodiment of the Supreme Guru, is portrayed here as trying to establish a basis for a relationship with his disciple. The disciple is a finite ego-centered human being, who lives, acts and reacts in the mundane plane. Action, matter and humanity are not necessarily opposed to the Divine according to the Gītā. But what man does or does not do with his socio-physical existence does matter. As long as man accepts his ego consciousness to be the center of human existence and he rejects or ignores the Divinity in him which constitutes by far the greater part of his totality there cannot be a foundation upon which the guru-disciple relationship can be built.

The Gītā plainly expects man to accept his totality. His ego consciousness, with its activities, must not be renounced. The domination, however, of the ego over man's total being must cease. Man, through his entire conscious efforts, must place his activities at the service of the Supreme Self. He must renounce only the desire and fruits of action but not action itself. All his activities must be offered as sacrifice to the Divine. Aurobindo considers sacrifice to be a universal law. In reference to the significance of sacrifice to bring about an optimum relationship between the ego and the Self he says:

> The acceptance of the law of sacrifice is a practical recognition by the ego that it is neither alone in the world nor its chief in the world. It is its admission that . . . there is beyond itself and behind that which is not its own egoistic person, something greater and completer, a divine ALL which demands from it subordination and service . . . The law of sacrifice travels in nature towards its culmination in the complete and unreserved self giving; it awakens the consciousness of the common self in the giver and the object of the sacrifice. This culmination of sacrifice is the height even of human love and devotion when it tries to become divine; for thèse the highest peak of love points into a heaven of complete mutual self giving, its summit is the raptuous fusing of two souls into one. This profounder idea of the world wide law is at the heart of the teaching about works given in the Gītā; a spiritual union with the highest by sacrifice, an unreserved self giving to the Eternal is the core of its doctrine.[6]

Accepting sacrifice as an established law in the universe may be quite a controversial matter for modern science. Accepting, however, this premise of sacrifice, the unreserved self giving to the Eternal, as a most remarkable functional insight would present no difficulty to analytical psychologists. It would be understood as man consciously, through his ego, is committed and involved in this sacrificial process, this unreserved self giving; and that when man uncompromisingly places his ego in the service of the Self there is sooner or later an awakening or what Jung frequently called a self-recollecting, that connects, unites and optimally relates the giver with the object of his sacrifice, or in other words, the ego with the Self.

According to Jung the act of making a sacrifice consists in the first place of giving something which belongs to oneself. When one gives something of his away what he gives is a symbol; and owing to his unconsciousness of its symbolic character, it adheres to his ego which is a part of his personality. If it is to be a true sacrifice, the gift must be given as if it were being destroyed. Only then is it possible for the egoistic claim to be given up. Yet looked at in another way this intentional loss is also a gain, for if one can give himself it proves that he possesses himself. Nobody can give what he does not have. It is in this way a conscious and deliberate self-surrender, proving one in control of his ego. In Jung's own words:

> The ego thus becomes the object of a moral act, for "I" am making a decision on behalf of an authority which is supraordinate to my ego nature. I am, as it were, deciding against my ego and renouncing my claim. The possibility of self-renunciation is an established psychological fact . . . it means that the ego is a relative quantity which can be subsumed under various supraordinate authorities . . . The conscious mind does not embrace the totality of a man, for this totality consists only partly of his conscious contents, and for the other and far greater part, of his unconscious, which is of indefinite extent with no assignable limits . . . Hence it is quite possible for the ego to be made into an object, that is to say, for a more compendious personality to emerge in the course of development and take the ego into its service. Since this growth of personality comes out of the unconscious, which is by definition unlimited, the extent of the personality now gradually realizing itself cannot in practice be limited either. But unlike the Freudian superego, it is still individual. It is in fact individuality in the highest sense.[7]

Since the Self suppresses the claim of the ego and compels one to make the sacrifice, in that sense the Self is the sacrificer and the ego is the sacrificed gift, namely, the human sacrifice. Jung further clarifies the meaning of sacrifice when he describes the relation of the ego to the Self as being like that of the son to the father.[8] He explains that the Self calls us to sacrifice ourselves like carrying out the sacrifice on itself. From sacrifice we gain what we give, which is ourselves. We gain freedom from unconscious projection and pass from unconsciousness into consciousness, from potentiality into actuality. Unconscious self sacrifice is merely an accident. The integration of the Self takes place by conscious assimilation of the split-off contents.

It can be clearly seen here that there are considerable similarities between the Gītā's message on the importance of carrying out action as a spontaneous sacrificial offering to the Divine, and Jung's formulations on sacrifice as a self-renunciation, in which the conscious ego renounces its claim and places itself into the service of the Supraordinate Self.

The Gītā recommends proper involvement in action. It states that activity is indispensable. No one should try to escape from conscious activity and awareness. When activities or works are offered to the Lord of sacrifice, then knowledge of the opposites is developed. The seeker learns to discriminate between essentials and unessentials. He begins to deal with these pairs of opposites which in a sense are challenging and tormenting his being in the battlefield of human existence. As the process continues and the sacrifice is subsumed at a higher level, the merging force of devotion, that subliminal emotional force of love for the Divine, fuses, unites and ideally relates the devotee with the Lord, the Supreme Guru Himself. Unreserved self giving of all conscious involvement in action; offering all knowledge emerging in and out of the battlefield of living; and finally pouring from the depths of the heart all zest and feeling of devotion, love and affection into the Divine lantern of sacrifice that contains the eternal flame of wisdom lit and burning; these are the tools of the Guru in the Gītā and the very basis for the sustaining relationship between him and his disciple.

The Gītā is constantly pointing out and emphasizing the need for the relationship between the finite seeker and the Divine Guru. Krṣṇa, the Supreme Self, is incarnated in a human body; he descends into human life and is intimately concerned with the personal disciple. Arjuna, the chosen disciple, despite his ignorance or through struggling with it is just as much concerned to ascend into the Godhead. There is here a dynamic process, a movement that brings together the ego conscious seeker from below with the transcendent wisdom of the Supreme Self from above. The optimum communication, relatedness and union between the finite disciple and the Supreme Guru (Ch. XVIII: 53-57) are the major objective and goal of the Gītā.

The essential thing to be understood is that there must be a Self, an ego and an established relationship between the two if there is to be Self-realization in the language of the Gītā or Individuation in the language of Analytical Psychology. When the ego is unrelated to the Self in human experience and reality, there is no actual guru and no disciple or in Jungian terms no actual analyst and no analysand. When the ego-Self relationship is initiated then there is a dynamically experienced relationship between guru and disciple or analyst and analysand. When the ego-Self relationship reaches an optimum state then, figuratively speaking, the guru and the disciple are one. This implies that the disciple is now the guru himself, or the analysand becomes himself the analyst of the Individuation process. Self-realization at this stage still carries on because according to the Gītā and Jung it is not a static but an on-going, dynamic process; at its center there is always the Eastern or Jungian guru and some place by its periphery there is always an ego conscious disciple. The Self-realizing human being is at once the gift and the sacrificer, as well as the disciple and the guru.

Chapter IV

SRI AUROBINDO'S VIEWS
ON THE GURU

Without indications of any major differences Sri Aurobindo expounds and elucidates the role of the guru according to traditional Eastern views. He goes further, however, to show how the concepts of the guru-disciple relationship apply even to modern man regardless of the complexities found in the contemporary world. In explaining the need for a guru he states that the spiritual progress of most human beings demands an extraneous support, an object of faith outside of us. The Hindu discipline of spirituality provides for this need of the soul by the conceptions of (1) the Ishta Devata, the chosen deity, not some inferior power, but a name and form of the transcendent Universal Godhead—it is necessary for some to conceive God in their own image or in some form beyond themselves, but consonant with their highest tendencies and seizable by their feelings and/or intelligence; (2) the Avatār, who is the Divine manifest in a human appearance such as Kṛṣṇa or Buddha or as a less marvelous intermediary like a prophet; and (3) the ordinary human guru who provides the seeker symbolically with a living relationship to the Divine.[1]

The guru may sometimes be the Incarnation or World Teacher, but it is sufficient that he should represent to the disciple the Divine Wisdom or make him feel the realized relation of the human soul with the Eternal.[2] Aurobindo frequently refers to the Supreme Guru as the Godhead, Divine, Spirit, World Teacher, Master, Supreme or Secret Guide or plainly Self. In connection with his own Integral Yoga teachings he says:

> As the supreme Shastra (knowledge of the truths, principles, powers and processes that govern the realization) of the integral Yoga is the eternal Veda secret in the heart of every man, so its supreme Guide and Teacher is the inner Guide, the World-Teacher, jagad-guru, secret within us. It is he who destroys our darkness by the resplendent light of his knowledge ... He discloses progressively in us his own nature of freedom, bliss, love, power, immortal being. He sets above us his divine example as our ideal and transforms the lower existence into a reflection of that which it contemplates. By the inpouring of his own influence and presence into us he enables the individual being to attain the identity with the universal and transcendent.[3]

More detailed explanation of Aurobindo's outlook on the guru will be discussed in this chapter.

The Significance of the Divine Birth

One of the basic premises of Integral Yoga is the Divine Birth with its two aspects of ascent and descent. It is described as a process in which the Godhead descends in man while man ascends into the Godhead. When Aurobindo says, "He who chooses the Infinite has been already chosen by the Infinite", he implies that the former cannot independently take place without simultaneous corresponding occurrence on the part of the latter.[4] There is a link that connects the finite man with the Infinite Self. The Divine Birth signifies the Union of these two with the resulting transformation as man's transcendent-spiritual rebirth.

The two aspects of the Divine Birth can best be explained through the Eastern concept of Avatarhood which was briefly introduced previously. The descent is characterized through the birth of God in humanity, the Godhead manifesting itself in the human form and nature. The ascent is described as the birth of man into the Godhead, man rising into the divine nature and consciousness (mad-bhāvan āgatah); it is the being born anew in a second birth of the soul. It is the new birth that Avatarhood is intended to serve.[5] The Divine takes upon himself the human nature with all its outward limitations and makes them the means and instruments of the Divine essence and power, a vessel of the Divine Birth and Divine works.

Extending the application of the ascending and descending aspects of the Divine Birth to any spiritual attainment situation is extremely helpful in understanding Aurobindo's basic formulations regarding the guru's role in Self-realization or in what he often calls emergence in Integral Perfection.

The Meaning of Spiritual Instruction and Attainment

According to Integral Yoga nothing can be taught to the human mind which is not already concealed as potential knowledge in the unfolding soul of man. Whatever perfection the outer man is capable of performing, it is only realizing the perfection of the Spirit because humans are already that in their secret nature. In this sense all teaching is a revealing, all becoming is an unfolding. Self-attainment is the secret and in increasing consciousness is the means and the process.

The usual means for this revealing is the word or thing heard (śruta). The word may come from within or from without, but in either case, it is an agency for setting the hidden knowledge to work. The word within may be the utterance of the inmost soul in us which is always open to the Divine or it may be the word of the Guru, the Universal Teacher, who is always seated in the hearts of all. The word from without representing the Divine as an aid in the work of Self unfolding may be either a word from the past or the more powerful word of the living human guru.[6] In other words the Supreme Teaching and the Universal Teacher are one existing within each man as a latent potential or in what psychologically is called an unconscious state. The internal and external word is the means by which the Teacher-Teaching communicates with the disciple and Self unfoldment begins to take place.

Self Consecration and Overall Attitude of the Sādhaka

Aurobindo stresses that all Yoga is a new birth; it is a birth out of the ordinary living conditions of man into a higher consciousness and greater and more divine being. But there must be an awakening to the necessity of the larger spiritual existence. The soul that is called to this deep and vast change may arrive in different ways at the initial departure. Regardless of the way it comes, there must be a decision of mind and will, a complete self consecration. To put it more descriptively in Aurobindo's own language:

> The acceptance of a new spiritual idea-force and upward orientation in the being, an illumination, a turning or conversion seized on by the will and the heart's aspiration − this is the momentous act which contains as in a seed all the results that the Yoga has to give. The mere idea or intellectual seeking of something higher beyond, however strongly grasped by the mind's interest, is ineffective unless it is seized on by the heart as the one thing desirable and by the will as the one thing to be done. For truth of the spirit has not to be merely thought but to be lived, and to live it demands a unified single-mindedness of the being; . . . He who seeks the Divine must consecrate himself to God and to God only.[7]

If the call to the change is sudden and overpowering then the Inner Guide, The Supreme Guru, is already at work although He may not necessarily manifest Himself yet in the person of His human representative. In many cases the call and the response to the change are slow and gradual and only eventually the impact may become adequate. If one wishes to respond adequately to the call and not merely progress slightly towards it, there must be an entire self-giving. But there must be meaning, clarity and awareness as to what and to whom one consecrates that which he calls 'himself'. This is how Aurobindo deals with the problem:

> For we have set out to conquer all ourselves and the world for God; we are determined to give him our becoming as well as our being and not merely to bring

the pure and naked spirit as a bare offering to a remote and secret Divinity in a distant heaven or abolish all we are in a holocaust to an immobile Absolute. The Divine that we adore is not only a remote extra-cosmic Reality, but a half-veiled manifestation present and near to us here in the universe. Life is the field of a divine manifestation not yet complete; here, in life, on earth, in the body, — ihaiva, as the Upaniṣads insist, — we have to unveil the Godhead; here we must make its transcendent greatness, light and sweetness real to our consciousness, here possess and, as far as may be, express it.[8]

Consecration is described here as a basic attitudinal commitment to the Highest Life and Realization on the part of the disciple. It is something that must be understood and dealt with in the initial stages although it is an ongoing experiential disposition. At times it may be used synonymously with sacrifice although in most profound Eastern writings sacrifice to the Divine implies a more specific activity or involvement in giving. Some of Aurobindo's most essential conclusions regarding the meaning of sacrifice are discussed in the chapter on "The Guru-Disciple Relationship in the Bhagavad Gītā."

Aurobindo, like most Eastern teachers, places great importance on the over-all attitude of the disciple toward the Master, as the Supreme Guru. The sādhaka (disciple in the path of yoga) is reminded that he has no business with pride or egoism because all is done for him from above, so he also has no right to despond because of his personal deficiencies or the stumblings of his nature. For the Force that works in him is impersonal — or super-personal — and infinite.

The sādhaka of Integral Yoga must not only show readiness but also be prepared to accept fully the essential role and authority of the Supreme Guru. He must recognize him as the inner Guide, the Master of Yoga, as Lord and as enjoyer and goal of all sacrifice and effort. It is immaterial whether he is first seen as an impersonal Wisdom, Love and Mover behind all things, as an Absolute, manifesting in the relative and attracting it, as one's highest Self and the highest Self of all, as a Divine Person within us and in the world, in one of his or her numerous forms and names or as the ideal that the mind conceives. In the end he is perceived as all and more than all these things together.[9] These thoughts are expressed as guidelines for the disciple and as an attempt to point out the nature and direction of his commitment. They are intended for an initial and continual impact upon the sādhaka's attitude and not as a prerequisite or as a fixed measure of attitudinal mode at any given point of his development.

The Approach of the Human Guru

The human teacher or guru of Integral Yoga will follow as much as he can the method of the Supreme Teacher or Guru:

> He will lead the disciple through the nature of the disciple. Teaching, example, influence, — these are the three instruments of the Guru. But the Teacher will not seek to impose himself or his opinions on the passive acceptance of the receptive mind; he will throw in only what is productive and sure as a seed which will grow under the divine fostering within. He will seek to awaken much more than to instruct; he will aim at natural process and free expansion. He will give a method as an aid, as an utilizable device, not as an imperative formula or a fixed routine. And he will be on his guard against the mechanizing of process. His whole business is to awaken the divine light and set working the divine force of which he, himself, is only a means and an aid, a body or a channel.[10]

The role of the human guru is viewed as that of a man who has established a functional relationship with the Divine, or the Collective Unconscious of Analytical Psychology, and is himself involved in the process of Integral Perfection or the parallel Jungian process of Individuation.

Great attention is given to the individual nature and needs of the disciple rather than applying fixed formulas and methods for everyone. Through his relationship with the sādhaka the human guru attempts to be instrumental so the latter may also establish a living relationship with the Divine and follow his own process of Integral Perfection. Aurobindo explains in some detail the meaning and use of the human teacher's three major instruments, namely: instruction, example and influence. Of these, the first considered in connection with its ordinary usage is merely the imparting of specific subject matter information and is the simplest to understand and apply. It is, however, the least meaningful and productive. Regarding the other two, Aurobindo states:

> The example is more powerful than the instruction; but it is not the example of the outward acts nor the personal character, which is of most importance . . . but what will stimulate aspiration in others is the central fact of the divine realization within him (the human guru) governing his whole life and inner state and all his activities. This is the universal and essential element; . . . Influence is more important than example. Influence is not the outward authority of the Teacher over his disciple, but the power of his contact, of his presence, of the nearness of his soul to the soul of another, infusing into it, even though in silence, that which he himself is and possesses. This is the supreme sign of the Master. For the greatest Master is much less a Teacher than a presence pouring the divine consciousness and its constituting light and power and purity and bliss into all who are receptive around him.[11]

These are the statements of a modern Eastern sage based on his philosophical and religious studies and primarily on his own spiritual experiences and insights. The language used is not expressed in psychological terms and there are certain metaphysical assumptions that the psychologist examines only for their psychological significance. Nevertheless, these formulations on the role of the Divine and human guru and disciple correspond appreciably to some of the findings based on the empirical investigations of Analytical Psychology. In the next section of this study some of these similarities will be brought out and the guru-disciple relationship will be more specifically compared with the Jungian analyst-analysand relationship.

Comparative Comments on Aurobindo's and Jung's Views

The significance of the Divine Birth that Aurobindo stressed definitely has its parallel in Analytical Psychology. The alchemical production of the lapis through the union of the opposites represents man's spiritual rebirth, the birth of the Self as the Divine Child. The opus is a process of individuation, of becoming a Self.[12]

Jung and Kerenyi elaborately explain the significance of the Divine Birth. They trace the Divine Child motif in myths of many nations and at various historical periods.[13] There are secondary variations or modifications in some of the motifs examined but they all point to the Divine Child as representing the birth of the Self through the union of the Divine with the human or more broadly, the union of the Spirit with nature.

Aurobindo speaks of the Spirit as being the source of all knowledge and wisdom. Human knowledge, he says, is not invented but is discovered. Man through the essence of the Spirit within him has potential access to Divine knowledge. Through the unfoldment of his soul this knowledge can be revealed and brought to awareness, thereby increasing his consciousness.

Jung, using different terms, basically agrees with this premise. He frequently indicated or said that the Collective Unconscious is the matrix of all instinctive knowledge and wisdom.[14] He spoke of the need and desirability of establishing a relationship with the unconscious allowing in this way, among other things, the knowledge and wisdom of the Collective Unconscious to become accessible to the ego consciousness. Both Jung and Aurobindo imply a dynamic process through which the wisdom of the unconscious is revealed, communicated, and assimilated-transformed into and through the human consciousness.

Aurobindo says that the teaching or revealing that is and comes from the Divine is accomplished by the means of the word, which may come from inside or from outside. The word, in other words, is the tool and means through which the guru reaches the disciple and knowledge becomes realizable. The word is a symbol that has meaning to human consciousness. The instinctive undifferentiated wisdom of the unconscious, through the word as expressed by Aurobindo or through what Jung discovered in his investigations as Logos, becomes incarnated, differentiated, expressed and fulfilled in human experience.[15] It is the word that makes the dialogue between the guru and the disciple meaningful and productive, whether it be the dialogue between the Divine Guru of the Gītā and his chosen disciple, or that of a more ordinary human guru and disciple of the East, or the analyst and analysand of Analytical Psychology.

Referring to the attitude of the disciple, Aurobindo stressed the seriousness and nature of the involved commitment. He spoke of the need for a total, unreserved and consciously executed self consecration to the Divine Guru if Self-realization is not going to be just a hobby or a secondary objective in the sādhaka's life. Jung also emphasized the need for dedication and unreserved offering of the ego as a sacrifice to the Self. To put it in psychological terms, the analysand must consciously offer his ego as a sacrificial gift to the Self without any strings attached to the offering. It must be a conscious commitment, otherwise it cannot be a genuine consecration of the ego to the service of the Self. In the chapter "The Guru-Disciple Relationship in the Bhagavad Gītā" some of Jung's views were presented regarding sacrifice and the depth of the commitment on the part of those approaching Individuation.

Aurobindo descriptively speaks of how the guru of integral yoga should function. He says that the human guru will follow as much as possible the methods of the Divine Teacher. In summary he mentions three basic tools: (1) instruction; (2) example; and (3) influence. Instruction which is given by means of verbal communication regarding the deeper truth is useful but the least effective of the three. Example, particularly not the outward acts but the basic character and personality of the teacher, is more effective. Influence, however, is the most effective and deals with the power of the contact, nearness and presence of the soul of the teacher and that of the disciple in relation to the great Soul. Finally, the guru recognizes and deals with the individual nature and needs of the seeker and applies no fixed formulas.

Jung, in his own psychological language, would greatly agree with this approach. Speaking of the role of the analyst's character and the influence that can be exerted as a result of his personality, the following statements of Jung bear much similarity to those of Sri Aurobindo:

Indeed, it is to a great extent immaterial which technique he uses (the doctor-psychotherapist), for it does not depend on "technique" but primarily on the personality who uses this method . . . The personality of the patient demands the personality of the doctor and not artificial technical procedures . . . He (psychotherapist) must be absolutely clear that the treatment of the soul of a patient is a relationship in which the doctor is just as much involved as the patient. A real treatment of the soul can only be individual, and, therefore, even the best technique is of purely relative value. But the general attitude of the doctor is all the more important, and he must know enough about himself to ensure that he will not destroy the particular qualities — whatever these may be — of the patient entrusted to him . . . A therapist who has a neurosis does not deserve the name, for it is not possible to bring the patient to a more advanced state than one has reached oneself . . . A doctor always has to do with the real man, who remains obstinately himself until the nature of his reality is recognized in its completeness. True, education can' proceed only from naked reality, not from any ideal illusion about man, however attractive . . . But if the doctor wishes to help a human being, he must be able to accept him as he is. And he can do this only when he has already seen and accepted himself as he is . . . I would even say that the practice of psychoanalysis requires not only psychological skill but above all a serious effort on the part of the doctor to develop his own character.[16]

Insight into one's own personality and a reasonable degree of Self-integration is required by both the integral yoga teacher as well as the Jungian analyst. In reference to the importance of accepting and dealing with the uniqueness and individual needs of the disciple, Jung says the following about the analysand:

When we are dealing with the human soul, we can only meet it on its own ground, and this is what we have to do when we are faced with the real and overpowering problems of life.[17]

Jung points out the meaning and significance of the human contact feeling that somewhat relates to the influence of contact described by Aurobindo as an instrument in the human guru-disciple relationship. In Jung's words:

> As long as you feel the human contact, the atmosphere of mutual confidence, there is no danger; even if you have to face the terror of insanity, or the menace of death, there is still that sphere of human trust, that certainty of understanding and of being understood, that belief that both will persist, no matter how dark the way.[18]

Jung is speaking of the analyst as a human guru who has established a meaningful and functional relationship with the Unconscious, an integrated person whose profession is to be instrumental in the healing of human psychic suffering and in the transformation and Individuation of the personality. Although many of the quotes attributed to Jung deal with the practice of healing the neurotic or psychotic person, the same principles apply to the main issue that concerns both Aurobindo and the Analytical Psychologist and that is helping human beings to become whole or integrated.

Chapter V

RAMAKRISHNA,
THE GREAT DEVOTIONAL GURU

Ramakrishna, a nineteenth century saint from Bengal, was a most unusual man. During the rather short span of his life he was at times considered by both strangers and intimates as a mad or insane person. During his later years he was revered by many as a most profound sage and was even proclaimed by eminent religious leaders and scholars as a genuine incarnation of God, an Avatār like Kṛṣṇa, Christ, or Buddha.

As a guru of men and one in his own right, Ramakrishna made a tremendous contribution in demonstrating the value of bhakti (devotion) as a psychic alchemical instrument in the Self-realization process. He showed through his own experiences and through his relationships with others how human emotions emerging from the depths of man's psyche can be transformed from gross or ordinary instinctual impulses into a creative, purposeful and self fulfilling flow of energy.

Although a study of the life of Ramakrishna would be of great psychological value, the scope of this investigation is restricted to those aspects of his life dealing with and clarifying the guru-disciple relationship.

In this chapter an examination will be made regarding: (1) the personal development and unusual experiences of Ramakrishna; (2) the psychological significance of Ramakrishna's experiences as a devotee: (3) the role of bhakti (devotion) in the guru-disciple relationship and (4) Ramakrishna's approach in his role as a guru.

The Tormented Searching and Attainment of the Devotee

From early childhood there was something unique or, at least, appreciably different in Ramakrishna's emotional makeup and his ways of expressing and dealing with feelings. According to biographical information, at the age of six or seven, while walking by a path between some fields, he saw in the sky a beautiful thunder-cloud which spread and covered the whole sky and a flight of snow white cranes passed in front of it. The beauty of the contrast apparently overwhelmed him and he was found there later unconscious by some villagers who carried him home.

At age nine he was asked to portray Śiva in a religious play. He fell into a strange mood that at first impressed the audience as quite a remarkable impersonation of God Śiva, Himself; but soon afterwards the play had to be interrupted because the boy's mood persisted and he remained in that subjective state overnight. About this time he was allowed to worship the Family Deity, Raghuvir. He was noticed then for the first time to begin to lose himself in contemplation while worshipping the stone image of Raghuvir.

The same year he organized, with the help and participation of his young friends, a dramatic group that held its performances at a nearby mango orchard. The themes acted out were selected from the famous Indian epics, the Ramāyāna and the Mahābhārata. "His favorite theme was the Vrindāvan episode of Krsna's life depicting those exquisite love-stories of Krsna and the milk maids and cowherd boys."[1]

It should be noted that shortly before Ramakrishna's birth his father, while away on a pilgrimage to Gaya, had a dream in which the Lord Vishnu promised to be born as his son. Also the mother in the village temple of Śiva had a vision indicating that she would give birth to a Divine Child. It should be remembered that in India the birth of a Divine Child, or Avatār, has been accepted for thousands of years as an incarnation of the Lord, the personal supreme God, in a human body, but it does not necessarily imply a virgin birth. It would be almost impossible to assess the impact of such tremendous personal experiences upon the parents, and if there were any suggestive communicated influences on the villagers, and if either or the combined reactions of the parents and the village folks had any significant affect on Ramakrishna's personality. These factors probably did have some influence in shaping the direction and outlook of his spiritual development. It should be kept in mind, however, that unless there were some unique and creatively intense elements within his own psyche, no suggestive or other external environmental influences could have brought out Ramakrishna's religious inspirational genius and spiritual attainment.

Sometime between his late teens and early adulthood Ramakrishna became a priest in charge of worship in the temple of Kāli at Dakshineswar, near Calcutta. His deep, devout attitude and character, as well as his strange unconventional manners became immediately noticeable to everyone around the Temple. He had a great yearning for a living vision of Kāli, the Mother of the Universe. He began to either forget or drop the formalities of worship and sitting by the image of the Goddess he sang rhapsodical devotional songs for hours. Sometimes in agony he rubbed his face against the ground and wept bitterly. In moments of skepticism he cried, saying: "Art thou true, Mother, or is it all fiction − mere poetry without any reality? If Thou dost exist, why do I not see Thee? Is Religion just phantasy and art Thou only a figment of man's imagination?"[2] Not long after, he had his first clear and vivid vision of the Divine Mother that he described in the following words:

> I felt as if my heart were being squeezed like a wet towel. I was overpowered with a great restlessness and a fear that it might not be my lot to realize Her in this life . . . Suddenly my glance fell on the sword that was kept in the Mother's temple. I determined to put an end to my life. When I jumped up like a madman and seized it, suddenly the blessed Mother revealed Herself . . . everything vanished from my sight, leaving no trace whatsoever, and in their stead I saw a limitless, infinite, effulgent Ocean of Consciousness. As far as the eye

could see, the shining billows were madly rushing at me from all sides with a terrific noise, to swallow me up! I was panting for breath. I was caught in the rush and collapsed, unconscious. What was happening in the outside world I did not know; but within me there was a steady flow of undiluted bliss, altogether new, and I felt the presence of the Divine Mother.[3]

After this experience his visions became deeper and more intimate. Even while fully conscious he would see Her (Divine Mother) tangibly as the temple, the trees, the river or the people around him. One day when the financial guardian of the temple property stepped in, he was profoundly moved by the young priest's devotion. He realized in a sense that Ramakrishna had transformed the stone image into the living Goddess.

One day Ramakrishna utterly shocked the temple-gardens manager when he fed to a cat food that was to be offered to Kāli. Regarding this incident Ramakrishna said that the Divine Mother revealed to him that it was She who had become everything. More specifically he added:

I found everything inside the room soaked, as it were, in Bliss − the Bliss of God. I saw a wicked man in front of the Kāli temple; but in him also I saw the power of the Divine Mother vibrating. That is why I fed the cat with the food that was to be offered to the Divine Mother. I clearly perceived that all this was the Divine Mother − even the cat.[4]

About this time Ramakrishna suffered from a severe burning sensation in his body. During worship, following the scriptures, he would imagine the "sinner" in himself and the destruction of this "sinner." One day while meditating he saw come out of himself a red-eyed man of black complexion, reeling like a drunkard. Soon there emerged from inside of himself another person, a serene countenance, a sannyāsi (Hindu Monk) carrying in his hand a trident with which he killed the dark complected man that had come out of him first. Immediately following this experience his pains and physical ailment disappeared.

The dramatic devotional expression of Ramakrishna's worship was not restricted to the Divine Mother. Around this time he worshipped God assuming the attitude that a servant has toward his master. He imitated the mood of Hanumān, the monkey chieftain of the Rāmāyana, the ideal servant of Rāmā. He lived on fruits and roots. He left a portion of his cloth hanging in the form of a tail, and when meditating on Hanumān, his movements and way of life began to resemble that of a monkey. He soon had a vision of Sītā, Rāmā's Divine consort, entering his body and then disappearing while saying, "I bequeath to you my smile."[5]

The young priest's behavior remained unconventional and he acted more and more strangely. One day while Rani Rasmani, the owner and benefactor of the temple, was listening to him sing during worship, he abruptly turned and slapped her because he sensed that she held unholy thoughts at the time. She apparently was thinking of a pending law suit. To the amazement of the bystanders, she accepted her punishment as if the Divine Mother, Herself, had imposed it. Mathur Babu, the temple property steward, was shocked. He and others attributed Ramakrishna's strange behavior, partially at least, to his observance of rigid sexual continence. They arranged for prostitutes to visit him and try to seduce him. They even took him to a house of prostitution in Calcutta. Ramakrishna only saw the Divine Mother in these, as in all women. Saluting Her presence, he went into samadhi (transcendent unconscious state). The women were profoundly moved by the experience and with tears in their eyes begged his pardon for having tempted him.[6]

These were only examples of Ramakrishna's unusual experiences and strange behavior. There were many more incidents of this sort that alarmed his relatives, friends and religious co-workers. Many of them doubted his sanity. He went back to his home village for a change of environment and he consented to get married. According to the Indian custom of child marriage, he was betrothed to a five year old girl. When she reached her teens, he lived with her for a time assuming a role that looked more like that of a father or brother and a teacher.

She accepted that relationship positively. The marriage was never, reportedly, consummated sexually.

Continuing with the biographical account of the period that he had returned to his native village, he remained there for approximately one and a half years. After some improvement in reference to his health, he went back to the temple at Dakshineswar. Soon, however, the symptoms of his earlier sickness and insane-like behavior reappeared in a more severe form. He started having the same old burning sensation in his body. He went into the same subjective ecstatic moods. He wept for hours at a time and had visions frequently. He started seeing the same sannyāsi who had in an earlier vision killed the sinner who came out of his own body. This time the figure of the sannyāsi was threatening him with the trident and ordering him to concentrate on God. On other occasions the same figure would visit distant places, following a luminous path and bring him back reports of what was happening there. Later Rama- krishna used to say that in the case of an advanced devotee, mind itself becomes the guru living and moving like an embodied being.

A nun known as the Brāhmani, a fifty year old woman adept in the Tāntrik and Vaishnava methods, came to Dakshine- swar and played an important part in Ramakrishna's life. She said that according to Bhakti scriptures, there were only two recorded cases in which the same kind of physical-emotional symptoms like Ramakrishna's had been experienced by the devotees while passing through the mahābhāva state, the most exalted rapture of Divine love. There are supposedly nineteen physical symptoms experienced during mahābhāva and shedding of tears, body tremors, horripulation, perspiration, and a burning sensation are among these. Listening to his experiences, responding to the effect of his presence and how others expressed that in his presence at times, or plainly touching his toes while in samadhi, they would temporarily feel being in a most insightful and lively state of realization, all these prompt- ed the Brāhmani to conclude that Ramakrishna was an Incarnation of God.

Mathur and others close to Ramakrishna doubted the conclusion that he was an Avātar, so two prominent pundits, one of which was the leader of the Vaishnava society, were invited to examine this matter. Both agreed that Ramakrishna had experienced mahābhāva and that was a sign of the rare manifestation of God in man, so they declared him an Avātar. Ramakrishna's reaction was that of relief to hear that his condition was not a disease. This event, outwardly at least, did not have any effect on his ways and outlook.[7]

Ramakrishna continued with his efforts to deepen his understanding of God and experience Him through various approaches. He now accepted the Brāhmani as his guru and started performing various Tāntrik rites and followed the disciplines of all sixty-four principal Tantra books; and it never took him more than three days to achieve the results promised in any of them. After the preliminary observances the whole world overwhelmingly appeared to him as lila, the Divine play of Śiva and Śakti, pervaded with Chit (Consciousness) and Ānada (Bliss). He acquired, according to recorded versions, supernatural powers of yoga that he spurned as of no value to the Spirit. He had a vision of how the Divine Māyā created, sustained, and absorbed into Herself the Universe. In this vision he saw a beautiful woman emerging from the Ganges and approaching his garden meditating grounds where she gave birth to a baby. She nursed it tenderly and a minute later she assumed a terrible aspect. She crushed it, swallowed it and re-entered the near-by waters of the Ganges.[8]

Following the completion of his Tāntrik sadhana (spiritual discipline) Ramakrishna under the guidance of the Brāhmani carried on with the disciplines of Vaishnavism, which attempts to develop the devotee's love for God by humanizing God. Here, "God is to be regarded as the devotee's Parent, Master, Friend, Child, Husband or Sweetheart, each correspondingly representing an intensification of love."[9] Ramakrishna had already practiced informally some of the devotional disciplines of Vaishnavism. He had worshipped Kāli as God in the form of his Mother and God as his Master when he assumed the personification of Hanumān, the monkey. With his demonstrated daring and persistent attitude, he completed the other phases of Vaishnavic devotional methods and as might be expected, he again had most unusual intense psychic experiences.

He was later initiated into the teachings of Advaita (non-dualist) Vedanta by a sannyāsi named Totapuri. Ramakrishna amazed his new guru with his remarkable progress. Following the Vedantic procedures he went into samadhi and remained in that state for three days. His guru is quoted to have said:

Is it possible that he has attained in a single day what took me forty years of strenuous practice to attain? Great God! It is short of a miracle.[10]

Finally with Totapuri's help Ramakrishna came out of samadhi.

Later Ramakrishna accepted a Moslem guru and with his assistance he prayed and practiced in other ways the religion of Islam. One of Ramakrishna's later disciples was well versed in Christianity. He became interested and started once again trying to experience God through the means of another religion. Each time he had psychic experiences corresponding to the form of the faith and doctrines that he practiced.

Ramakrishna learned through personal experience that God must be realized through the individual efforts of the sincere and persevering seekers, and that no one religion or method of spiritual attainment has an exclusive formula or claim to it.

The Psychological Significance of Ramakrishna's Experiences

In the preceding section a description was given of certain experiences of an almost illiterate peasant boy who had a passion to experience life as an on-going drama, made of emotion, to be constantly felt with the care, shaping and appreciation of an artist dedicating his works to the Divine. These unusual experiences, however, were often overwhelming. Considering that Ramakrishna for years had neither adequate nor reassuring help from a spiritual guide, nor the services of a truly competent modern psychotherapist, it is a small wonder that he did not succumb to these merciless forces of the Unconscious and become mentally crippled, or plainly insane, for the rest of his life. On the contrary, in many ways he appeared to have been able, in terms of Analytical Psychology, to deal with the activated contents of the Collective Unconscious and eventually make great strides in Self-realization.

At this point a question might be raised regarding the objective truth of certain events in Ramakrishna's life as recorded. Such a question, if not carried to extremes, would appear to be a crucial one if a psychologically meaningful evaluation of this man's unusual experiences is to be made. Attempting to answer this query, consideration should be given to the following factors: (1) although most of the biographical information was recorded by persons who were highly impressed with Ramakrishna, many unfavorable and perhaps even discrediting accounts were also inserted along with the favorable ones; (2) this is a biographical record of a man who lived most of his life during the second half of the nineteenth century, a not too distant period in history, making collaborating biographical evidence reasonably accessible to investigators; (3) Analytical Psychologists know through empirical investigations and through personally acquired experience that when the Collective Unconscious becomes constellated as in Ramakrishna's case, the archetypal activity is not carried on in a totally unpredictable manner − these archetypes are manifested by means of images which follow a meaningful pattern or sequential arrangement determined by personality characteristics of the individual and the way he reacts to these emotionally charged contents; and (4) even if the biographical material were disregarded as such, just the examination of the archetypal motifs and the individual reactions to these alleged experiences would be a worthwhile undertaking as an attempt to better understand the functioning of man's psyche.

Reviewing events during Gadadhar's (Ramakrishna's childhood name) early years, it can be noticed that he had by nature a beautiful voice and a spontaneous need to express his intense emotional nature dramatically and imaginatively. These qualities were particularly appreciated by the village women who began to treat him as if he were their darling boy. He received much attention and praise for singing religious devotional songs, by expressing feelings of affection openly, and by often acting out episodes from religious plays and giving a free flow to his imagination.

In Analytical Psychology such personality traits are associated with the "Eros Principle" which Jung explains as follows:

Woman's psychology is founded on the principle of Eros, the great binder and loosener, whereas from ancient times the ruling principle ascribed to man is Logos. The concept of Eros could be expressed in modern terms as psychic relatedness and that of Logos as objective interest.[11]

In Gadadhar's case there was an early tendency to respond to this feminine psychic relationship function. It could be said that with constantly reinforced influences surrounding him there was an overdevelopment of the Eros and an underdevelopment of the Logos functioning in his personality make-up.

Even using Jung's definitions of Eros and Logos one has to be extremely careful when applying them to a situation like Ramakrishna's. Cultural and other factors could complicate or confuse our understanding on this matter. For example, during boyhood and at later times Ramakrishna displayed much interest in carving various personified images of God, observing the ways that people dressed, walked, talked and expressed themselves. He noticed with keen interest minute objects in the fields, the ways of animals and even watched with wondering eyes the shape, color and movement of the clouds in the skies. It would certainly be incorrect to state that he did not show any interest in objects and the objective world. It would be, however, fair to state that Ramakrishna's interest and involvement in objects was one of a religious-artistic nature, which does correspond to the Eros-feminine psychic function principle.

Ramakrishna was not concerned personally with earning a livelihood. He early lost interest in school and had a distaste for intellectual undertakings. He was largely indifferent to the mundane strivings and accomplishments of society although he was most concerned and devoted to the spiritual needs and well-being of people as individuals and as an entire humanity. It would be fair to say that in many ways he did not display concern and involvement with the expectations and values of society in general, particularly when considered from a Western cultural point of view. It is in this sense that his development was one-sided and many of the neglected, purposely ignored, activities could be identified with the Logos function.

More specifically the question might be raised as to whether or not Ramakrishna had a mother complex and, if he did, in what negative or positive ways it manifested itself. From the viewpoint of Analytical Psychology, he appears to have had a strong mother complex. Although some of his personality disturbance symptoms during childhood and early adult years may be associated with this complex, and dealing with the anima in general, the predominant lasting effects were positive ones.

Jung indicates that typical psychopathological effects on the son having a mother complex are homosexuality, Don Juanism and sometimes also impotence. None of these, however, can be observed in the life of Ramakrishna. Some psychologists not trained to understand the symbolic meaning and transformation impact of religious devotion and other spiritual practices might insist that the biographical data suggests at least latent homosexuality. In addition to what already has been mentioned suggesting effeminate manners and attitudes, they might also refer to other recorded incidents. His rather frequent and remarkably successful impersonation of female roles in plays and for pranks would be an indication.[12] Another one would be the incident of a desire under the impulse of the female mood that used to arise in Ramakrishna's mind in his adolescent years. Like the gopis of Vraja, he used to think that he, too, would have been blessed to love and have Sri Kṛṣṇa as husband had he been born in the female form. Considering his male body as an obstacle in attainment of Sri Kṛṣṇa, he had a phantasy that if he were born again, he would become a beautiful child widow and would not know anyone except Sri Kṛṣṇa as husband; he would have a small piece of land, a cow and would cultivate the field to produce the necessities of living and devote himself exclusively to Kṛṣṇa who would come every evening for a visit and eat the sweet-meats that he made from the milk of the cow and other products of the fields. This marriage would have been sort of a secret between Kṛṣṇa and Ramakrishna. As a child bride of Kṛṣṇa, he would also have an elderly woman living with him as a guardian.[13]

It would be much more accurate to say that at certain times of his life, Ramakrishna, with an intense religious devotional longing, opened himself fully to the over-powering influence of the mother archetype. While he temporarily appeared to be possessed by the irrational archetypal forces, he was not actually just passively responding to them. His devotional appeal was to experience the true nature of the Divine Mother. His entire being was keyed up to penetrate beyond the shallow and dark regions of the unconscious and with as much clarity as humanly possible experience the very nature of the Great Mother, the transcendent God, and through such a union the very essence of his own nature. In his attitude there was submission to the archetypal forces and depths of the maternal unconscious, but at the same time there was determination to experience and deal individually with his relationship with the Mother-Father God. From early age, he was accustomed to accept the combined masculine-feminine attributes of God. He frequently said that when there is Kāli there is immutably Śiva. There cannot be the one without the other. On one occasion he tried to illustrate this point by saying, "Śiva, Kāli, and Hari (a name for Vishnu) are but different forms of the One. He is blessed, indeed, who has known all as one."

> Outwardly he appears as Śiva's devotee. But in his heart he worships Kāli, the blissful Mother and with his tongue he chants aloud Lord Hari's name.[14]

The statement dealing with the unity behind the various aspects of God has been repeatedly emphasized in Indian religious and philosophical writings. The remarks about the devotee's approach to knowledge and experience of this unity could be interpreted psychologically as an intuitive understanding that Śiva, the masculine aspect of Divinity, deals with the outward conscious shaping and development of man; that Kāli, the Eternal Feminine, deals with the inward essence of man that can be reached through the heart, through feeling; and through Hari, the personified Vishnu, the devotee's appeal is made by chanting the name, the word, the Logos aspect that makes things conscious. In other words, this is an appeal for ultimate Self-integration.

Jung states that if the "mother complex" concept is taken out of its narrow psychopathological setting, it can be seen that is has positive effects as well:

> Thus a man with a mother complex may have a finely differentiated Eros instead of, or in addition to, homosexuality. (Something of this sort is suggested by Plato in his Symposium.) This gives him a great capacity for friendship, which often creates ties of astonishing tenderness between men and may even rescue friendship between the sexes from the limbo of the impossible. He may have good taste and an aesthetic sense which are fostered by the presence of a feminine streak. Then he may be supremely gifted as a teacher because of his almost feminine insight and tact. He is likely to have a feeling for history, and to be conservative in the best sense and cherish the values of the past. Often, he is endowed with a wealth of religious feelings, which help to bring the ecclesia spiritualis into reality; and a spiritual receptivity which makes him responsive to revelation.
>
> In the same way, what in its negative aspect is Don Juanism can appear positively as bold and resolute manliness; ambitious striving after the highest goals; opposition to all stupidity, narrow mindedness, injustice, and laziness; willingness to make sacrifices for what is regarded as right, sometimes bordering on heroism, perseverance, inflexibility and toughness of will; a curiosity that does not shrink even from the riddles of the universe; and finally a revolutionary spirit which strives to put a new face upon the world.
>
> All these possibilities are reflected in the mythological motifs enumerated earlier as different aspects of the mother archetype.[15]

Proceeding with the hypothesis that Ramakrishna had a mother complex and attempting to examine it psychologically in the light of Jung's findings regarding the mother archetype many things in Ramakrishna's life that appeared strange, confusing, and in some respects alarming, begin to make sense.

With his highly developed Eros function he was noted for his talent of making friends and being liked by most of those who made his acquaintance. He was well known for his spiritual devotion, receptivity to Divine revelation and his simple, lively and verbally picturesque ways of instruction. He had a great talent for listening to historical, religious-literary works and retaining them with remarkable accuracy while being inspired by them. He was not sexually impotent, nor was he an overt or latent homosexual. He was apparently among those rather few who do not have a need to express their sexuality through physical media. He did not seek to suppress or repress his sexual needs. He, instead, sublimated them, but not in the Freudian or in some other Western form of sublimation which is achieved by means of forcing the will to turn one's attention and energies into socially valued non-sexual activities. Neither did he use hatha yoga methods of sublimation. It was through his dramatic, passionate devotional activities that he sublimated his sexual drive. Despite the anxiety and pains that he suffered during the periods of his unguided devotional excesses, he was by all indications eventually able to transmute his emotional-sexual longings into a dynamically blissful experience of communion with the Divine. In psychological terms, he was able to experience the unity within his self, or the wholeness or fullness, or uniqueness of his self.

Jung's investigations provide us with valuable information regarding the activities of the instincts in relation to the Eros theory. He states:

> Although the strongest instincts undoubtedly require concrete realization and generally enforce it, they cannot be considered exclusively biological since the course they actually follow is subject to powerful modifications coming from the personality itself. If a man's temperament inclines him to a spiritual attitude, even the concrete activity of the instincts will take on a certain symbolical character. This activity is no longer the mere satisfaction of instinctual impulses, for it is now associated with or complicated by "meanings." In the case of purely syndromal instinctive processes, which do not demand concrete realization to the same

extent, the symbolical character of their fulfillment is all the more marked. The most vivid examples of these complications are probably to be found in erotic phenomenology. Four stages were known even in the late classical period, Hawwah (Eve), Helen (of Troy), the Virgin Mary, and Sophia . . . The nomenclature shows that we are dealing with the heterosexual Eros — or anima — figure in four stages, and consequently with the four stages of the Eros cult. The first stage, Hawwah, Eve, earth — is purely biological; woman is equated with the mother and only represents something to be fertilized. The second stage is still dominated by the sexual Eros, but on an aesthetic and romantic level where woman has already acquired some value as an individual. The third stage raises Eros to the heights of religious devotion and thus spiritualizes him; Hawwah has been replaced by spiritual motherhood. Finally, the fourth stage illustrates something which unexpectedly goes beyond the almost unsurpassable third stage: Sapientia. How can wisdom transcend the most holy and the most pure? — Presumably only by virtue of the truth that the less sometimes means the more. This stage represents spiritualization of Helen and consequently of Eros as such.[16]

In reference to Jung's four stages of the Eros cult, it appears to this writer that Ramakrishna's relationship to the anima was in many ways at the third, the Mary-spiritual motherhood stage, and probably sometimes in view of his tremendous experiences at the fourth, the Sophia-wisdom stage. It would be almost impossible to distinguish when he was exactly relating at the third or the fourth stage, but it would suffice to state that his anima relationship contained characteristics of the Spiritual Mother and the Wisdom stages. Such an inference can be made by examining various incidents in his biography, particularly some of his visions and similar psychic experiences. For example the impact of his first clear and vivid vision of the Divine Mother, described in the preceding section of this study, seems to have components of both the Mary and Sophia stages of the relationship to the anima. Devotionally and in desperation he appealed for a direct experience to know the true nature of the Divine Mother. He appealed as a devoted spiritual child.

Psychologically, he was actually opening himself to the over-whelming activated forces of the Collective Unconscious. The Great Mother archetype did present itself in imagery making her nature and presence felt in the psyche of the devotee. What he experienced was the anima as an effulgent ocean of conscious-ness and its shining billows madly rushing at him and him falling blissfully in ecstasis; and though unconscious of his ordinary state of being, he could keep feeling the undiluted flow of the bliss, altogether new and constantly moving. With his devotional attitude he was psychologically seeking and in many ways responding to the Mary stage of anima relationship. But when inwardly, intensely, and most deeply he sought to know the Mother, the anima archetype presented its deeper aspects, the Sophia elements, which in the vision could be detected through the elements of the effulgent ocean of consciousness, etc.

It should be kept in mind that although a man may relate to the anima at one or more stages of the Eros cult, the archetype, nevertheless, contains the combined elements and total nature of the four stages. For a particular person the symbolical meaning of the experiencing may be at a certain stage, but *various multi-stage* attributes of the archetype may at times be seen in the fantasies or dreams of such a person. For example, in one of Ramakrishna's later visions, described in the preceding section of the study, the anima appeared emerging from the Ganges in the form of a beautiful woman with its birth-giving, life-sustaining qualities, its terrible-devouring aspects and even-tually disappeared into the waters of the Ganges, the abode of Her transpersonal nature. This is an archetypal experience communicating not one but most of the essential aspects of the anima. It is quite impressive how the anima did manifest Herself in a personally meaningful manner and reveal Her major aspects. That is precisely what is meant psychologically to establish a relationship with the anima or other pertinent archetypal forces instead of remaining unconscious of them and allowing them to affect us in autonomous psychic complexes.

Continuing with Jung's observations on how men with a mother-complex may be affected in positive ways, he spoke of what amounts to Don Juanism in reverse. Many of the qualities listed appear to correspond with Sri Ramakrishna's personality traits. His resolute manliness, uncompromising striving after the highest, ignoring narrow-mindedness and unconventionally displaying toughness of will, and readiness to sacrifice for the sake of spiritual realization, all these were typical attributes of his character.

In examining some of the negative mother-complex effects, one could elaborate on the consequences of Ramakrishna's unbalanced personality development. In many ways he showed lack of adaptation in taking care of his physical needs. He often was not aware as to whether or not he had eaten or if it were day or night, even when the candles were lit for the evening. From the time he was born until he died, others were looking after his physical and sociofinancial needs. For years his nephew, Hriday, was purportedly attending closely after his bodily needs. Those near to him often scheduled a good many of his external activities. He never, however, allowed others to interfere with his spiritual devotion, initiative and determination. Some psychologists would, in this regard, say that Ramakrishna's behavior shows strong signs of infantilism. If such a statement were qualified to mean that in the sociophysical areas which he deliberately chose to ignore he did not develop beyond the infantile-childhood stage, then such a statement would be correct. No generalization regarding his total personality development should be made on the basis of such an observation. That would be a most misleading oversimplification. In terms of Jung's types and functions it would appear that feeling and intuition were highly developed while sensation and thinking were neglected or undeveloped. He was most likely an introvert.

Much attention has been given so far to show how Ramakrishna dealt with the anima, since some of his greatest problems and achievements were greatly affected by his initial disposition as well as his later encounter with the anima. It is well known, however, that before much progress can be made toward Individuation one must deal first with the persona and the shadow which are, so to say, layers of the personality located at a more shallow level than the anima, in reference to proximity to ego consciousness. In this section a few relevent comments will be made regarding how, apparently, Ramakrishna dealt with the persona and the shadow. His continual attitude of responding to the inward impulses and dictates of his nature even at the anticipation of subsequent social disapproval and personal discomfort is an indication that there were no appreciable persona interference signs in his psychological and spiritual development. A good illustration of this point is the incident of insisting upon and actually accepting alms from a sudra (low caste) woman during the ceremony of investiture with the sacred thread despite the initial shock and extreme objections of his Brāhmana caste family members.[17] His ignoring the conventional modes of worship while officiating as a priest in the Temple of Kāli and carrying on with behavior that deprecated his social image and status in the eyes of most of those surrounding him, is another of many instances in which persona-dominating factors did not interfere with the urge to Self-realization.

A good example of how Ramakrishna dealt with the shadow was described in the preceding section. In one of his visions during the early years at the Temple in Dakshineswar, he saw a man with dark complexion come out of himself, reeling like a drunkard. Immediately afterwards a sannyāsi also came out of himself and with a trident that he was carrying, attacked and killed the dark complected shadow-like figure. Considering that Ramakrishna, just before having the vision and in accordance with scriptural injunction, was imagining the sinner in himself, he apparently had an insight into the dark or shadow-like side of his nature which emerged out of him as a personified visual figure. The subsequent killing of this shadow aspect probably represented the killing or effective dealing with the hidden dark and undesirable aspects of his personality. It is interesting to note that immediately following this experience he was cured from severe burning sensations that he had had for some time in various parts of his body. The vivid experience of dealing with the shadow element psychically appeared to have occurred at the same time that the body dealt with the burning-sensation illness, as if there were an existing psychosomatic, synchronistic (meaningful coincidence) relationship between the two events.

Subsequent experiences that occurred a few years later and which were also mentioned in the preceding section of this study, are noteworthy in reference to Ramakrishna's progress in dealing with the shadow. The same sannyāsi who had previously killed the dark complected figure began to appear again, now threatening Ramakrishna himself and demanding that he put forth more effort and show more earnestness in his search for God. This psychic figure gradually assumed the role of a personified psychic guru who in various ways instructed him. It can be seen here that the sannyāsi figure replaced the dark shadow figure of the earlier days and now began to exert an influence of a positive shadow in addition to other symbolic positive roles that he assumed as Ramakrishna continued to probe more insightfully into the depths of the Unconscious.

Referring to the guru role that sometimes fantasy figures assume, Jung had some similar experiences. In one of them he speaks of Philemon, a pagan-like old man with the horns of a bull holding four keys and having the wings of a kingfisher. He first appeared in a dream and as Jung pursued the image in fantasy, the figure continued to appear. In his biographical notes Jung remarked:

> Philemon and other figures of my fantasies brought home to me the crucial insight that there are things in the psyche which I do not produce, but which produce themselves and have their own life . . . In my fantasies I held conversations with him, . . . He (Philemon) said I treated thoughts as if I generated them myself, but in his view thoughts were like animals in the forest, or people in the room . . . It was he who taught me psychic objectivity, the reality of the psyche . . . Psychologically Philemon represented superior insight. He was a mysterious figure to me. At times he seemed to me quite real, as if he were a living personality. I went walking up and down the garden with him, and to me he was what the Indians call a guru.[18]

Such experiences seem to reflect a certain level of psychic development in which there exists a suitable relationship between ego consciousness and the Unconscious. When there is sufficient readiness, Jung's method of active imagination is quite helpful in communicating meaningfully with figures of one's own fantasies.

One of the dangers that exists when the Collective Unconscious is activated is that the individual may identify with its contents as if he, himself, were the possessor of the Collective Psyche and in this way he becomes what Jung calls "psychically inflated."[19] It would be extremely difficult to determine with confidence whether or not Ramakrishna was psychically inflated during temporary periods of the earlier years of his search. There is some evidence, however, that during most of his adult years he was spiritually modest and did not identify consciously with the Collective Unconscious in any manner suggesting inflation. The following example shows how Ramakrishna was careful not even to accept claims that others would make regarding his being an Avātar. Once a host of his stated: "You, too, are that same Rāmā." Ramakrishna's reply was: "For heaven's sake! Never say that. . .

'That Rāmā dwells in all beings; He exists every-where in the universe.' I am your servant. It is Rāmā, Himself who has become all men, animals, and other beings.[20]

During the same occasion he further demonstrated his humility as well as his honest confident feelings when the host told him: "You are free from love and hatred." Ramakrishna replied: "How so? I engaged a carriage to bring me to Calcutta and advanced the coachman three ānnās. But he didn't turn up. I became very angry with him. He is a very wicked man. He made me suffer a lot."[21]

In a similar way Sri Ramakrishna dealt with his disciples when they expressed that he was an incarnation of God. He reminded them that years previously when learned pundits declared him an Avātar he did not let that get to his head, and he was not prepared to get excited just because they expressed the same views with conviction.

Ramakrishna's Approach In His Role As A Guru

Although Ramakrishna as a devotee and guru emphasized full-hearted devotion to God, he did not use bhakti as an exclusive method to spiritual attainment. Neither did he attempt to instruct and guide all his disciples in the same manner. For instance, he encouraged and, with subtle insistence, persuaded Vivekananda, who initially objected, to study and practice the teachings of Vedanta. At this time, however, he positively did not allow his other devotees to do likewise.

> Thus although Swami Vivekananda and other boy devotees sat and slept, ate and walked together, and discussed religious theories together in the company of the Master (Ramakrishna) at Dakshineswar, the latter was training them all in various ways according to their peculiar taste and turn of mind.[22]

In this respect, both Ramakrishna and Jung are in agreement that the urge to Self-realization depends on the individual temperament and makeup of each person and no one method is suitable for every aspirant.

On various occasions Ramakrishna pointed out that it is a most difficult task to be a genuine teacher and very few attain the necessary qualifications to carry out the responsibilities of such a position. He frequently indicated that a human guru never ceases being a śiṣya of the Supreme Guru. Years after he had completed different forms of sadhana (spiritual discipline) he would still explain that his attitude toward God as the Guru was that of a child toward his mother, or that of a servant toward his master, or that of a lover toward his or her loved one. The following quotation illustrates many of the aspects of the point just made:

> Do you know my attitude? As for myself, I eat, drink and live happily. The rest the Divine Mother knows. Indeed, there are three words that pick my flesh: 'guru,' 'master,' and 'father.' There is only one Guru, and that is Satchidānanda. He alone is the Teacher. My attitude toward God is that of a child toward its mother. One can get human gurus by the million. All want to be teachers. But who cares to be a disciple? It is extremely difficult to teach others. A man can teach only if God reveals himself to him and gives the command. . . . Unless you have a command from God who will listen to your word? God does reveal

Himself to man and speaks. Only then may one receive
His command. How forceful are the words of such a
teacher! They can move mountains. But mere lectures?
People will listen to them for a few days and then forget
them. They will never act upon mere words. To teach
others one must have a badge of authority; otherwise
teaching becomes a mockery. A man who is himself
ignorant starts out to teach others — like the blind
leading the blind. Instead of doing good, such teaching
does harm. After the realization of God, one obtains an
inner vision. Only then can one diagnose a person's
spiritual malady and give instruction . . . without the
commission of God, man becomes vain.[23]

In addition to showing how a human guru should relate to
the Supreme Guru, here Ramakrishna stresses that it is *this very
relationship* which makes the difference between an ordinary
human being and a teacher of men. In psychological language it
would be the same as saying that the psychotherapist as a
healer, or guide, or teacher, in reference to the psyche, may
have the right and necessary ability to practice his profession
adequately only when he, himself, has undergone analysis and
has established an on-going relationship with the forces and
wisdom of the Unconscious. Jung also makes great demands
upon the integrity and personality development of the psychotherapist:

The doctor is, therefore, faced with the same task
which he wants his patient to face . . . The doctor must
consistently strive to meet his own therapeutic demand
if he wishes to ensure the right sort of influence over his
patients. All these guiding principles of therapy make so
many ethical demands which can be summed up in the
single truth: Be the man through whom you wish to
influence others. Here talk has always been counted
hollow, and there is no trick, however artful, by which
this simple truth can be evaded in the long run. The fact
of being convinced and not the thing that we are
convinced of — that is what has always, and at all times,
worked. Thus the fourth stage of analytical psychology
requires the counter-application to the doctor, himself,
of whichever system is believed in — and moreover, with
the same relentlessness, consistency, and perseverance

with which the doctor applies it to the patient . . . who can educate others if he is himself uneducated? Who can enlighten others if he is still in the dark about himself? And who (can) purify others if he himself (is) impure?[24]

Ramakrishna in a religious context speaks of the teacher's need for inner development and on-going self education so he can experience the depths of the psyche and truly communicate the language and reality of the Unconscious through the medium of his teaching. Jung arrives independently at the same conclusion, speaking in relation to the self-education needs of the psychotherapist and healthy people as well. In sort of a summation he makes the following far-reaching remarks regarding the new role of Analytical Psychology:

What was formerly a method of medical treatment now becomes a method of self-education, and with this the horizon of our psychology is immeasurably widened. The crucial thing is no longer the medical diploma, but the human quality . . . analytical psychology has burst the bonds which till then had bound it to the consulting room of the doctor. It goes beyond itself to fill the hiatus that has hitherto put Western civilization at a psychic disadvantage as compared with the civilizations of the East. We Westerners knew only how to tame and subdue the psyche; we knew nothing about its methodical development . . . It seems to me that the findings of analytical psychology can at least provide the foundation, for as soon as psychotherapy takes the doctor, himself, for its subject, it transcends its medical origins and ceases to be merely a method for treating the sick. It now treats the healthy or such as have a moral right to psychic health.[25]

Here Jung explained how Analytical Psychology, from a specialty treating the psychologically ill, became a scientifically oriented system for dealing with the self-education or psychic development needs of the healthy. As he pointed out, this approach was not new to the East; but it was a remarkable achievement for the West. At this point, what is more remarkable is the similarity of the conclusions arrived at by

Jung, a medically trained psychotherapist, and Ramakrishna, a predominantly self-taught religious devotee and guru. Although both of them frequently and abundantly quoted various human authorities and resources, they strongly emphasized the primary authority and resource as being the psychic reality that can be known only through personal experience.

Ramakrishna was noted for his broad-minded outlook regarding the teachings of different religions. He frequently stated that sincerity and intensity of one's commitment in worshipping and experiencing God was the main thing. According to one's development and needs he would respond to such particular religious practices suitable to his situation. One of the contributions attributed to him was his spontaneous conclusion, and dynamic way of propounding, that "all faiths are true – as many faiths, so many paths."[2 6]

There has been traditionally more inter-religious and interdenominational tolerance in India than in many other parts of the world. Yet, Ramakrishna's liberal religious views and attitude had much of an impact in his country. Ramakrishna used to mix freely and enjoy the company of sadhus (holy men) of various religious backgrounds. He was much disappointed, however, with the narrow-minded attitude that they displayed, avoiding the fellowship or even looking down at sadhus of different religious orientations.

Although there are many methods of spiritual realization, and he saw merits in all of them, he saw none surpassing bhakti. His experiences, gestures, manners, thoughts, words, singing, dancing and everything about him was a living testimony of how devotion as activated-emotion penetrated the depths of his being and enabled him to know God, or in psychological terms, to experience the uniqueness and wholeness of his nature.

When he speaks of devotion he speaks of feeling that is activated by irresistible yearning for God. As was briefly mentioned earlier in this study, Ramakrishna practiced the various modes of devotion to God, such as the kind that a child has toward a loving mother, or a servant toward a most revered master, or a lover toward her beloved, like the love of the gopis of Vrindāvan, and particularly Rādhā for Krsna. Drawing apparently from his own experiences as well as from the bhakti teachings of the Vaishnavas or the Tāntriks, he made practical suggestions by giving vivid examples of how such practices can be carried out. When some of his disciples once asked him how one can develop real love for God, he replied by relating the story of a sage who, when asked the same question, took his disciple into the river and dipped his head under the water, holding it there for some time. Finally the disciple in desperation was able to get his head back to the surface and breathe. Then Ramakrishna emphatically added that one must prompt himself to experience with the same desperate urgency and with the same realism the feeling of love for God.

He was once asked under what conditions one sees God. He replied:

> Cry to the Lord with an intensely yearning heart and you will certainly see Him. People shed a whole jug of tears for wife and children. They swim in tears for money. But who weeps for God? Cry to Him with a real cry . . . Longing is like the rosy dawn. After the dawn out comes the sun. Longing is followed by a vision of God . . . The point is to love God even as the mother loves her child, the chaste wife, her husband, and the worldly man his wealth. Add together these three forces of love, these three forces of attraction, and give it all to God. Then you will certainly see Him . . . It is necessary to pray to Him with a longing heart. The kitten knows only how to call its mother, crying, "Mew, Mew!" . . . But as soon as the mother hears this cry, wherever she may be, she comes to the kitten.[27]

On this occasion, as on so many others, Ramakrishna urged a purposeful stirring up of one's emotions. Everyone has strong feelings from time to time, but what he recommends is not to leave emotional experience to random conditions. He reminds aspirants that they do have in their disposition something familiar, simple and most powerful. They all know how to feel. It is not a matter of learning complicated or confusing skills or dealing with the uncertainty of vague abstract ideas. To express emotion is something that men do from infancy through old age. What they so often overlook is the overwhelming impact that emotions have upon their entire well-being. Ramakrishna, as a master in the methods of bhakti, is more or less saying to let loose of one's emotions. One should express them as intensely as he possibly can even if it takes weeping in desperation and shedding tears of hope, anticipation, joy and fulfillment; one should give free play to his feelings; he should not be afraid of letting them out, regardless of what they are, as long as he keeps one indispensable thing in mind – to offer these unleashed yearnings to the Altar of the Highest. All these evoked emotions should be nothing less than one's conscious commitment to reach the depths of his being and experience union with God.

It appears that this devotional approach of generating emotion, with the earnest intent of transforming it into an experience of union with the Divine within, may often have the effect of activating the Collective Unconscious. For persons with unstable personalities or whose religious zeal may be expressed in ambivalent ways, there is a possible danger of not being able to deal with the dark aspects of the activated Unconscious. Such practices sometimes may produce emotional disturbances or even mental breakdowns. For the average, sincere devotee who depends upon bhakti practices to some extent, but does not remain exclusively dependent upon emotional expression as a means of responding to religion and life in general, devotion may become a most productive instrument in his search for wholeness.

In a way, bhakti is like psychic fire. Physically burning fire has been a most useful implement assisting man to evolve from a gross animal level into a highly rational and cultured being. Likewise emotion, as psychic fire or energy, may be instrumental in the psychic transformation of man, assisting him to evolve into an integrated human being. Fire, whether it be burning as a physical fuel or as generated emotion, if improperly used may cause damage or even severe destruction. Chaudhuri clearly and precisely discusses the basic advantages and disadvantages of bhakti techniques. It would be beyond the scope of this study to summarize his ideas on this matter. It will suffice, however, to quote a few pertinent points that he makes:

Until and unless devotion is consummated in authentic spiritual enlightenment, the danger is always there. Spiritual enlightenment, variously designated as bodhi, prājnā, nirvanā, satori, cosmic consciousness, etc., is a radically different dimension of experience beyond the intellectual and emotional functions of the mind. It is reflected on the mental level as the harmony of love and wisdom.

Another danger inherent in the purely devotional approach is the undermining of practical efficiency. The more a person allows himself to be carried off by waves of emotion, ecstasy and rapture, the more incapacitated he becomes in the practical field. He shouts and sings in joy, he rolls on the floor, he dances in a mood of frenzy. He sweats and trembles, and he may repeatedly fall into swoons. All such emotional agitation or holy-rollerism pretty soon brings about nervous exhaustion.

In the interest of the integration of personality it is desirable that the influx of emotion occasioned by spiritual practice should be turned into calm creative energy. The intensified devotion, the exuberance of love and joy, has to be properly channeled under the guidance of some socio-ethical or humanitarian or culturally creative purpose of existence. Emotion is energy. But energy needs to be informed with a definite practical end in order to be productive.[28]

It was mentioned earlier that Ramakrishna, at certain periods of his life, engaged in excessive, frenzy-like devotional activities; but eventually he broadened his spiritual outlook and engaged in a variety of spiritual disciplines. As a guru he stressed what might be called his own unique sort of an eclectic approach in which bhakti had a prominent position and jnāna (knowledge of God arrived through reasoning and discrimination) had at times an important and at other times a secondary place. He explained that for most persons bhakti was a simple, safe and adequate approach to spiritual attainment. He often seemed to have intuitively deep psychological insights. He appeared in many ways to be aware of what Jung calls psychic reality and psychic objectivity.[29] This is apparent in his statements (below) in which he tries to explain the psychological reality of one's individuality, and the reality of God in his various forms when experienced by a human being. He additionally compares some aspects of the Vedantic system with those of the bhakti method and stresses the psychological and religious simplicity and value of the latter, particularly when applied to the majority of aspirants:

> The real nature of Brahman cannot be described. But so long as your individuality is real, the world also is real, and equally real are the different forms of God and the feeling that God is a Person.
>
> Yours is a path of bhakti; that is very good; it is an easy path. Who can fully know the infinite God? And what need is there of knowing the Infinite? Having attained this rare human birth, my supreme need is to develop love for the Lotus feet of God.
>
> If a jug of water is enough to remove my thirst, why should I measure the quantity of water in a lake? I become drunk on even a half a bottle of wine — what is the use of calculating the quantity of liquor in the tavern? What need is there of knowing the Infinite?
>
> The various stages of mind of the Brahma jñāni (knower of Brahma) are described in the Vedas. The path of knowledge is extremely difficult. One cannot obtain jñāna if one has the least trace of worldliness and the slightest attachment to 'woman or gold'. This is not the path for the Kaliyuga (the current one of the four world periods according to Hindu writings.)[30]

In the example given below, Ramakrishna seems to be reacting to immensely felt archetypal forces evoked by reciting a passage from the Bhagavata Purana dealing with the Vrindāvan episode. It is shown how he utilized that occasion to explain instructionally the psychic reality, meaning and value of the experience. While speaking to his disciples, he said:

> You must feel love for Him (God) and be attracted to Him. The gopis of Vrindāvan felt the attraction of Kṛṣṇa. Let me sing you a song:
> Listen! The flute has sounded in yonder wood.
> There I must Fly, for Kṛṣṇa waits on the path.
> Tell me, friends, will you come along or no?
> To you my Kṛṣṇa is merely an empty name;
> To me He is the anguish of my heart.
> You hear His flute-notes only with your ears.

But Oh, I hear them in my deepest soul.
I hear His flute calling: Rādhā, come out;
Without you the grove is shorn of its loveliness!

Ramakrishna sang the song with tears in his eyes, and said to Keshab and the other devotees:

Whether you accept Rādhā and Kṛṣṇa or not, please do accept their attraction for each other. Try to create the same yearning in your heart for God. Yearning is all you need in order to realize Him.[31]

Once his beloved disciple Vivekananda challenged him regarding the historicity of the play of Rādhā and Kṛṣṇa at Vrindāvan. Ramakrishna responded by taking the position that anything that is experienced psychically is historically as real as any physical occurrence. In his exact words he said:

Very well, let us take for granted that there was never any one called Sri Rādhika, and that some loving sādhaka had an imaginary conception of Rādhā's personality. But while picturing that character, the sādhaka, you must admit had to lose himself completely in Sri Rādhā's mood, and thus he became Rādhā. It is, therefore, proved that the play at Vrindāvan was thus enacted in the outer world also.[32]

Ramakrishna's reply also suggests how much importance he placed on the role and value of imagination. Jung places great importance on the role of imagination. At certain stages of personality development he recommends active imagination in which a person concentrates upon the objects of his fantasies and has a dialogue with the fantasy figures. It is an attempt to bring into consciousness, by means of assimilation, the symbolic urges and hints of the Unconscious. Many passages in the biography indicate that Ramakrishna used active imagination extensively. His later confrontations and guru-like relationship with the sannyāsi figure that had originally come out of him, and certain of the dialogues that he had and kept with the Divine Mother for years, seem to point out the active imagination approach of dealing with the Unconscious.

With Jung, active imagination is an advanced technique of dealing with one's unconscious contents. Speaking more broadly on the value of imagination, he said:

> Truth to tell, I have no small opinion of fantasy. To me, it is the maternally creative side of the masculine mind. When all is said and done, we can never rise above fantasy. It is true that there are unprofitable, futile, morbid, and unsatisfying fantasies ... but the faulty performance (of fantasy) proves nothing against the normal performance. All the works of man have their origin in creative imagination ... The creative activity of imagination frees man from his bondage to the "nothing but" (explaining something unknown by reducing it to something apparently known and thereby devaluing it) and raises him to the status of one who plays. As Schiller says, man is completely human only when he is at play.[33]

Jung, by encouraging his students and patients, when they reached a certain stage of development, to express themselves by means of brush, pencil or pen, expected such activity to produce an effect. When one struggles for hours with refractory brush and colours, or shaping words, in prose or in verse, only to produce at the end something which at face value is perfectly senseless, and yet be willing to carry on with the same type of activity time after time, the fantasy one is acting upon does not strike him as senseless. As he is working at it there is an increased effect upon him. He is not a passive bystander. Through his involvement, the concrete shaping of the image enforces a continuous study of it in all its parts and so it develops its effects more fully. In this way the patient becomes considerably independent of the analyst, because what he paints or writes are active fantasies within him but no longer in the guise of his previous error, when he mistook the personal ego for the Self. His ego now appears as the object of that which works within him. This newly won independence is a step toward psychological maturity.[34]

Ramakrishna dramatically spoke of the multi-faceted aspects of devotion to God. At face value, one might conclude that he spoke of somehow rousing certain feelings and emotional reactions. A closer examination will show that the devotional approach relies very heavily on imagination. Without the play of imagination, feeling can hardly emerge. In addition to the typical forms of bhakti already mentioned, Ramakrishna actively dealt with fantasy or other imagination-associated activities in many incidental day-to-day occurrences. Although not continually, at certain early and later periods of his life, he much enjoyed engaging in the making and painting of various clay images of God. It seemed to have a pronounced effect upon him. Even when not worshipping, the casual listening to the recitation of religious epics or devotional songs would often produce an active, imaginative involvement and response on his part.

As a teacher, he used simple and descriptive language often in a parable-like narrative fashion. His choice of words, phrases and statements appeared to be imaginatively inspired and with the very intent of stirring the imagination and feelings of the listener. It is interesting to notice that in his presence, while watching him and listening to him, even persons who thought he was insane or a fraud would be much moved and impressed. Somehow they would sense his active and physically charged relationship with what Jung calls the Collective Unconscious and often they were tangibly touched by witnessing such an experience even though they did not know how to account for it. Some of the scholarly Brāhmo Samāj (an Indian Theistic-humanistic organization) members who made his acquaintance reacted in that way. Even Ramakrishna's cousin, a priest in one of the temples at Dakshineswar, experienced the same thing. When away, he had serious doubts about Ramakrishna's sanity and religious development. In his presence all the doubts would disappear and he would declare that Ramakrishna had the most profound spiritual insights and was a highly evolved soul.[3][5]

Much has been said about how Ramakrishna dealt with fantasies and visions while awake, semi-conscious, or in a state of samadhi. Very little, however, has been written regarding his dreams and his attitude toward them. Perhaps the reason is that he was so sensitively aware of the psychic reality of internal experiences that he did not often consider it necessary to qualify which of his psychic experiences occurred while physically asleep or during a full or borderline awakened state. In any case, he did seem to take dreams seriously.

One time he asked a devotee if he had dreams. It is not indicated whether he was one of his own or one of so many strangers visiting from time-to-time at Dakshineswar. The subsequent conversation would rather suggest that he was one of the latter kind. The devotee replied affirmatively and narrated a recent strange dream that he had. He saw the whole world enveloped in water. There were a few boats there but huge waves sank them. He was ready to board a ship with some others when a brāhmin came walking over the expanse of water. The devotee asked him how he could do such a thing and the reply was that under the water there was a bridge. The devotee wanted to accompany the brāhmin who was going to Bhawāni-pur, the city of the Divine Mother. Right then Ramakrishna interjected, "Oh, I am thrilled to hear the story!" The devotee finished by saying that the brāhmin was in a hurry and could not wait for him to come out of the ship, but told him to remember this path and come after him. Ramakrishna's final recorded remark was, "Oh, my hair is standing on end! Please be initiated by a guru as soon as possible."

Examining briefly this dream and the circumstances in connection with it from the viewpoint of Analytical Psychology: The Great Mother motif appears first in Her cataclysmic aspect (flood). Later it is shown that through discriminating knowledge, symbolized by the brāhmin, there is a bridge and a path that leads to the centre or ultimate aspect of the Great Feminine, which here is represented by the city of the Great Mother. The highest aspect of the Feminine Principle is Sophia and on various occasions She is associated as the Goddess of the City, the protector and promoter of human culture and development.[36] Undoubtedly, as Jung would insist, there were many personal elements that would have to be elucidated through the cooperation and involvement of the dreamer. Even at the archetypal level there are other implications that could not be discussed here because of the limited scope of this study. It is important, however, to note that Ramakrishna not only reacted with intense interest but he also indicated that he was listening to a dream that to him was a story. Very likely he was responding to the apparent archetypal elements in the dream. On that basis he expressed his deeply felt conclusion that the dream was hinting that the devotee needed immediate and serious spiritual guidance and that initiation by a competent guru was the first step to this objective. Most Jungian analysts probably would not quarrel with such an interpretive conclusion; but as indicated previously, they would also encourage the dreamer to personally reflect, deal with and react to the contents of the dream. The basic premise would be that even if the guru's or analyst's interpretations were adequate, unless *the dreamer* arrived at some awareness and meaningfulness of the interpretation, the dream explanations would be of little or no value.

What should not be overlooked, however, is that Rama-krishna was supposedly able to tune-in through his highly developed Eros (the Jungian Eros) function and interact meaningfully with others even in many non-verbal ways. His understanding and communication with others was often much more deep and elaborate than what ordinarily might be expected. Throughout the biography there are many instances when strangers or devotees felt that Ramakrishna was actually reading their minds and he was speaking directly to them about their specific problem or situation even though there might be others present at the time and he was addressing a group. Some might explain it by means of intuition. Others might say that he had that ability which some stage performers or speakers have to captivate their audience. Psychologically, the essential thing to consider is that he had a living connection with the Unconscious. Within the socio-religious environmental circle suited to his devotional introverted nature, he was able to relate his insights to those near and around him. What made him a great guru in the eyes and hearts of others was his penetrating insight into the depths of the psyche and his unreserved generous efforts to communicate and share what he spiritually had learned and mastered.

His sharing was a genuine one. He cared for his disciples. Long before they came to him he would burst into tears at night saying, "Come to me, my children; where are you?" He visualized the day when he would be involved in caring for his devotees and instructing each one according to his own special needs. There is psychologically an inestimable value in the power generated when one human being is in great need and another human being in the most genuine way cares to help and is actually able to help.

What is most important here is not necessarily the professed need, nor the professed caring and providing of help. What is most essential is the joint experiencing of the meaning of a felt need, the joint realization that the need can be met, that a joint effort is made to meet such a need, and that a mutual communication exists showing that it is fulfilling to meet such a need. In other words, sharing symbolically the meaning of a great need or aspiration and sharing symbolically the fulfillment of such need or aspiration is an awareness and solution-evoking process. Ramakrishna, in the area of spiritual needs, was noted for putting himself in the mood of the person he was trying to understand or help. He expressed empathy at a penetrating psychic level. With his intensely generated sincerity and confident intuitive understanding of human instincts, emotions and spiritual longings he had a most uplifting effect on his listeners, particularly those close to him.

An important issue that often came up was whether or not a householder could attain spiritual realization since the very nature of his activities would not allow him to renounce the world fully and place himself totally in the service of God. When questioned on such matters, he often approached it similarly to the Gītā saying that if one dedicated his activities to God he would not be handicapped in making spiritual progress. He even added that most sannyāsis originally began through partial renunciation. On another occasion he replied in the following way:

> Why shouldn't one be able to realize God in this world? King Janaka had such realization. . .
>
> Janaka's might was unsurpassed;
> What did he lack of the world or the Spirit?
> Holding to one as well as the other,
> He drank his milk from a brimming cup!

> But one cannot be a King Janaka all of a sudden. Janaka at first practiced much austerity in solitude. Even if one lives in the world, one must go into solitude now and then.[37]

Ramakrishna was very tolerant with persons who had extreme moral weaknesses, if he felt that they were sincerely seeking God. He fully accepted as a disciple Girish Ghose, an actor, an alcoholic, a smoker of opium for fifteen years, who led sexually an illicit and immoral life, and was much disliked initially by the disciples. His relationship with Girish was cordial all along and he never tried to lecture him to mend his undesirable ways. He applied a psychological approach whereby Girish gave Ramakrishna the power of attorney. Apparently this reassured him and probably it appealed to his passive-dependency needs; but soon he found out that in a sense, it made him a slave to Ramakrishna. For example, when one day Girish said, "I shall do this," Ramakrishna corrected him saying, "You mustn't talk in that dogmatic way: Say 'I shall do this if God wills.' " Hence he tried to surrender his will altogether to Ramakrishna. He soon found out that the way of complete self-surrender in the religious life was harder than the way of self-reliance and effort.[38] Apparently he made significant progress in some areas of his spiritual development, although no detailed recorded information is available.

Ramakrishna did not have the training of a modern psychologist nor did he have the clinical knowledge of contemporary psychology, that in many cases alcoholics and habitual users of narcotic drugs have extreme passive-dependency needs. Although there were in India classical precedents regarding 'giving the power of attorney' practice, Ramakrishna chose to use it only with Girish Ghose, among his many close disciples and lay devotees. He used it with an intermittently highly successful and well known actor, outwardly defiant and unconventional, a person who according to surface appearances would be least amenable to such a submissively demanding approach. Yet that did not prevent Ramakrishna from applying his lay but keen psychological insight. He accepted the authority as well as the responsibility to deal with Girish as a guru and he persisted in it. With his unshaken accepting relationship he allowed the disciple's infantile dependency needs to be met at the psychic plane. He challenged the disciple to submit the ego to the Self. He helped him to develop a healthy appreciation of submission. He appealed to the emotional attraction of dependency by attempting to activate and bring about archetypal reactions whereby socio-emotional dependency could be transformed into spiritual dependency which eventually produces outward adequacy, assertiveness and initiative. With his disciple, Vivekananda, he recognized something that was much different. He noticed a keen intellect and unusual rational discriminating abilities. He encouraged these qualities, as briefly mentioned earlier, by applying Vedantic methods and was never perturbed when this disciple frequently challenged him argumentatively during discussions on various religious and social issues.

In conclusion, Ramakrishna, in many respects, had established a remarkable relationship with the Unconscious. He developed a great insight regarding the spiritual needs of human beings. He had a tremendous understanding regarding the emotional elements involved in human relationships. He neglected several aspects of his physical, social and intellectual development. As a guru he practiced what he preached. He submitted himself to the challenging and transformation producing confrontation with the forces of the psyche; and with the insight and authority gained by such experiences he became a guide, a teacher, and a great religious pioneering leader of men. He said:

> First of all set up God in the shrine of your heart and then deliver lectures as much as you like. . .
> First of all invoke the Deity, and then give lectures to your heart's content. First of all dive deep. Plunge to the bottom and gather up the gems. Then you may do other things.[39]

That is what he daringly and precisely did. Modern psychology, particularly through the approach of Analytical Psychology, can probably learn much by examining many of the creative, soul stirring attitudes and ways of his life. Even examination of some of the alarming consequences of Rama-krishna's one-sided development could be productive. But as Jung frequently cautioned, a study of Eastern approaches and contributions in the realm of the psyche should not be done with the intent of imitating the East but for the purpose of understanding and enriching our own heritage and Western outlook. [40] One might add that it should be for the purpose of hopefully reaching a meaningful synthesizing approach that combines the best of the East and the West.

Chapter VI

THE GURU-DISCIPLE RELATIONSHIP
IN THE LEGENDARY BIOGRAPHY OF
TIBET'S GREAT YOGI MILAREPA

Evans-Wentz, the editor of the English translation of the biography, indicated on various occasions that folklore had a significant influence in the writing of *Tibet's Great Yogi Milarepa*. In certain ways, however, he appears to accept as historical fact many of the incidents attributed to the personal life and experiences of Milarepa, the great Tibetan yogi and guru of the Kargyütpa Buddhist sect.[1] Regardless of how great or how little a role the historical person Milarepa has played in this biography, and regardless of where folk-lore and myth enter or stay out, this legendary narrative has had a most profound impact over the centuries. Even now, Milarepa has continued to be highly esteemed and venerated not only by the Kargyütpas but also by most people of different religious backgrounds in Tibet and other neighboring countries.

Certain teachings, traditions and attitudes regarding the guru-disciple relationship can be readily noticed in this bio-graphical work. Taking these factors into consideration, an attempt will be made here to examine the implications of such a relationship for the Jungian process of Individuation. The biography will be examined from the standpoint that the mythical, legendary and folk-lore elements in it have significant psychological meaning and value for modern psychology. Which aspects of Milarepa's life, if any, were historically factual will not be a concern of this investigation.

Initial Aspects of Milarepa's Journey

In Analytical Psychology the adventures and struggles that a mythical hero has while performing his heroic acts in order to attain his goal are known as "the journey of the hero" which represents the process of Individuation. As Jung and his co-workers often said, the hero only anticipates the later psychological development of humanity. Referring to the journey in general, Esther Harding said:

> In dreams and myths, as well as in parable and allegory, man's inner life and the process of his inner development is almost constantly represented as a journey, a progress from one stage to the next. On the way persons and adventures are encountered and a goal is envisioned which may or may not be reached, but whose attainment is thought of as the climax and fulfillment of life's effort.[2]

Some of the basic motifs in classical hero myths can also be found with certain variations in this narrative on the life of Milarepa. He, as the hero, is not associated with a miraculous birth or abandonment during infancy as has often been the case. As it happens in some myths, he was born to ordinary human parents. Early in childhood, however, his father died, leaving him an orphan and his mother a widow, a feature frequently noticeable in hero stories.

Milarepa was born in a small Tibetan town during the eleventh century, A.D. Through an oversight of his father, the family was deprived of its rather wealthy estate which was greedily taken over by Jetsün's (Milarepa's first name) paternal uncle and aunt. His mother became resentful because of the injustice done to her and her two children. She schemed to bring about revenge. When Milarepa reached his teens, she convinced him to go to a guru of the black arts and learn how to be a sorcerer so he could destroy the family enemies and thus avenge the honor of his father. As in the case of Odysseus, who accepted the call to go to Troy and help a comrade retrieve his kidnapped wife, Helen, Milarepa accepted the call to help in what was considered a culturally just and important cause. Through means of black magic, Milarepa brought about death and destruction to all those attending the wedding of his paternal uncle's eldest son. Only the uncle and aunt were spared, supposedly as a convincing testimony to them and others of the carried-out vengeance.

Milarepa's mother is described in a frenzy-like fashion, rejoicing at the news of this calamity. The town folk, who for years were sympathetic to her plight, observing her continuing morbid satisfaction over the outcome of her vindictive planning, now turn against her. Presumably for her safety and that of Jetsün, she writes and convinces him to produce a hail storm in his home town as a demonstration of his occult powers so no one would dare to harm him or members of his family. Once again Milarepa becomes an accomplice to his mother's vengeful schemes. Through further efforts, he learns how to produce hail storms and finally sets one upon his home village, destroying the rich crops of that year and causing much suffering and famine.

Through these activities Jetsün loses his innocence. He is no longer the well-meaning lad who set out to defend the honor of the family and comfort a justly suffering mother. Psychologically speaking, he is slowly coming out of his infantile unconsciousness. He has become aware of the opposites appearing as conflicting forces. He now perceives himself as an evil-doer who has taken many lives away and has additionally caused much damage to many innocent people. He is now a hated and a wicked person. He is left with two alternatives. He may either slide back into unconsciousness and not face the major challenge, remaining under the domination of the Great Mother archetype and fixated at or near an infantile state, or he may proceed with the journey. These two alternatives are only psychological ones because the narrative dealing with a hero myth leaves no room for such alternatives. A hero is only a hero because he undertakes the journey.

Milarepa is portrayed here as a doomed sinner. The colorful representation of rebirth in one of the Mahayanic hells that awaits him as the fate of the terrible evil-doer makes the taking of the journey most imperative. The legendary narration further dramatizes the urgency of his predicament. The reader is reminded that sages, great yogis and bodhisattvas must spend several incarnations on earth before they attain Buddhahood or complete liberation; yet Jetsün, in addition to accepting full responsibility for his redemption, must also accomplish this feat within one lifetime.

In a way, Milarepa's journey began when he set out to take revenge against his oppressive paternal uncle and aunt who represented the archetypal first parents. In hero myths, this corresponds to the slaying of the dragon in which both the First Parents, the Father and the Mother, must be slain. The slaying of the dragon does not stop at this level. At a later stage it assumes a new form and meaning which would be beyond the scope of this study to discuss here. It should be added, however, that the dragon of most myths guards what is frequently called "the treasure hard to attain," which represents the goal of the hero's journey.[3] In Milarepa's case, when he reached the stage of desperately seeking liberation, it could be said that the "treasure hard to attain" was what the biography repeatedly described as "finding and mastering the doctrine of liberation in one lifetime."

The Search for the Guru

In the preceding section, most compelling reasons were given in explaining why Milarepa had to seek ultimate liberation. The search for a guru that could help him attain such a monumental goal was also portrayed as a most difficult task.

Milarepa was not yet fully prepared for the challenge. He was seeking and hoping to find an easy solution. With the blessings and material support of his well-meaning guru of the black arts, he presented himself to a lāma (Tibetan priest or religious preceptor) who possessed the doctrine called "The

Great Perfection." He was readily accepted and initiated but after several days no signs of spiritual progress were evident. The explanation given was pride. Our novice chose to believe that he was one of those few gifted persons who by the mere hearing of the teachings would be delivered, and thus he failed to meditate and put the doctrine to the test of practice. The lāma plainly indicated that under such circumstances he would be unable to be of any help. He did, however, add that there was one who could help:

> He is the worthiest among the worthiest of men, a very prince among translators, — one who hath obtained supernormal knowledge in the new Tāntrik Doctrines, unequaled in all the three worlds; he is called Marpa, the Translator. Between thee and him there is a karmic connexion which cometh from past lives. To him thou must go.[4]

Milarepa's response was an inexpressible feeling of delight; an overwhelming sensation of thrill passed through his entire body. A most powerful expression of faith arose within him, and he set out with a single purpose in mind — to find his destined Guru.[5]

At this point, the deeper meaning of the guru-disciple relationship begins to unveil itself. When the śisya realizes that superficial involvement in religious instruction and initiations does not produce any essential degree of spiritual attainment and that only an uncompromising inner commitment is needed, then he is ready to tread the path that leads to the Supreme Guru who is nothing less than the Supreme Realization itself. On the human level of experience, something similar to Analytical Psychology's activation of the Collective Unconscious takes place. The śisya's readiness to deal with the demands of the Self-realization process also includes the anticipation of help forthcoming through the relationship with a competent and specially destined human guru. With this new remarkable attitude, the guru-disciple relationship has been already established psychologically. The socio-physical meeting with the guru and working out the details for initiation and upadesa are only a part of the psychic reality pattern that is unfolded before him.

It is interesting to notice that at this point the narrative introduces the explanation that there was a karmic connection, through previous births, between the great guru Marpa and the disciple-to-be, Milarepa. Regardless of the metaphysical implications of the statement, which will be ignored here, there is great psychological significance linking causally, in a personal way, the guru with the disciple. It helps both of them to accept more personal responsibility regarding their respective roles. The meaning of their relationship is accepted at a deeper level of psychic reality; it is not just a well-meant, conceptually perceived but psycho-emotionally uninvolved relationship and commitment.

It is worth noting that about the same time Milarepa was told that Marpa was the guru who could help him, there was a psychic connection between the two, and he experienced psychically the meaning of the anticipated relationship; Marpa and his wife separately had unusual dream experiences convincingly pointing to the forthcoming arrival of the heroic and most remarkable disciple, Milarepa.

Both dreams were quite descriptive and rich in symbolism and yet at a simple-to-understand Tāntrik Buddhist layman level. Both Marpa and his wife are much impressed by the unusual nature and importance of their dreams; but only Marpa, representing the consciously aware guru, understands objectively the meaning and interpretation. His wife has only strong intuitive hints regarding the meaning of her dream.

Responding to the hints and information in the dreams just mentioned, Marpa is shown preparing himself for a symbolic reception of his disciple-to-be. Although he had not plowed the fields for years, if ever, that morning he told his wife that he was going down the road to do some plowing and asked her to bring him some chhang (Tibetan beer). His wife unsuccessfully tried to dissuade him, explaining that it would be scandalous for a great lāma with so many laborers at his disposal to go plowing.

Milarepa had already set out to find his guru. He asked along the way, "Where doth the Great Yogi, Marpa the Translator live?" Nobody seemed to know Marpa, but finally one person indicated that thereabouts was one called Marpa, but he did not bear such a grand title of "Great Yogi, the Translator."[6] Probably a point is made here that the greatness of certain spiritual leaders is not often recognized by many ordinary people around them.

When Milarepa approached the area by the field which Marpa was plowing, the latter asked him who he was and what was his objective. Listening to the answer, Marpa asked Milarepa to finish plowing the field, offered him the jug of chhang that his wife had brought him and without revealing his identity, promised to procure an introduction to lāma Marpa for him. Jetsün, with delight, accepted the offer and with vigor plowed the field which was named "Aid Field" because of the symbolized aid it supplied the novice in meeting his guru.

It has been mentioned that Marpa knew in advance, psychically, about the arrival of Milarepa. He went out to welcome his prospective disciple by symbolically engaging in humble, hard and productively promising labor of plowing the field and sharing this labor with the arriving disciple, and also offering him chhang, the customary drink given to guests in Tibet. Yet Marpa did not utter a word to explain that he expected him. As if talking to any arrived stranger under similar circumstances, he offered Milarepa two alternatives: He would supply food and clothing and the novice was to seek spiritual instruction elsewhere, or he would assist with spiritual development and the disciple was to care for his own food and clothing. Jetsün accepted the second alternative.

It was much later, and only after the śiṣya completed his probationary period, that Marpa explained to Milarepa that he knew in advance about his coming and that he had the qualities for amazing and nearly unsurpassed spiritual attainment. This indicates that in some respects the Kargyütpa guru knew much about the meaning and value of psychic-reality experiencing and their application as well as limitation when related to physical reality experiencing. Marpa is portrayed as knowing that despite all the psychic prophetic omens regarding the spiritual greatness of Milarepa, the latter must consciously submit to all the painstaking tests of psychic development apprenticeship before the spiritual genius can fully manifest and prove itself. Lāma

Govinda elaborates on this point, explaining that the Buddhist yogi is not concerned with fixed physical and metaphysical interpretations of his meditative experiences. The following is what he says:

> In the Buddhist Tāntrik system the elements (earth, water, fire and air) are being more and more detached from their material qualities or from their natural prototypes. Their mutual relationship is regarded to be more important than their organic functions . . . (Buddhist yoga) does not start from static data which, once given, have to be adhered to rigidly, but from dynamic principles or possibilities of psychic transmutation. The Buddhist Tāntrik adept does not ask 'What is there?' but 'What can be made of it?'[7]

This is consistent with the basic Buddhist approach being a psychological one. By 'What is there,' customarily a speculative examination of the object is made. By 'What can be made of it,' an examination is made of the meaning of the object in relation to the experiencing subject which, when carried far enough, involves a transformation or transmutation process.

The Methods of the Guru and the Disciple's Attitude and Involvement

Milarepa was accepted as a śiṣya on a most severe and uncertain probationary status. As a novice, he must be tested under the most extreme conditions and must complete most challenging and demanding tasks. Some of these require the supernatural powers and endurance of a mythological hero. A Tāntrik Buddhist hero he is, and the symbolical adventures and fate of such a hero he must bear.

Jetsün, having accepted the responsibility of supplying his own bodily needs, went on an alms-collecting mission. When he returned with a sack of barley, he offered it to Marpa who at first scolded him harshly for the way in which he dropped the sack on the ground; and then in a whispering voice he blessed the disciple's offering. Throughout the probationary period, with a few exceptions, Marpa was treating Milarepa in a rude and sometimes abusive manner. He sent him out to make storms and use some of his other skills as a sorcerer. Upon completion of such deeds, contradicting himself, he blamed the disciple for doing such atrocious acts of killing people and causing great property destruction. He demanded that Milarepa restore the lives of those killed and the property destroyed. That placed Jetsün in a state of desperation because he did not have the power of performing such feats. He had come to the guru in the first place because he did not have the psychic power and insight to undo the damning effects of his previous deeds. The initial testing of the guru, expecting the disciple to supply his own food and clothing, probably represents the view that a sādhaka earnestly seeking spiritual attainment must not harbor attitudes and feelings of physical dependency or indifference in dealing with his personal needs. The guru's request and expectation that the disciple exercise super-normal skills to kill the unjust and destroy their property, and subsequently demanding that the disciple undo such evil acts probably represents the guru's concern to test the psychic abilities of the disciple and his ability to discriminate and assume moral responsibility for his actions.

Marpa left Milarepa only overnight to wrestle with the dilemma between restoring the lives of those he killed and the destroyed crops, or not receiving initiation and instruction in the doctrines of liberation within a lifetime. The next morning Marpa presented his disciple with an alternate task and upon its completion he promised to initiate him and instill the "Great Doctrine." He took him to a hilltop by the east and asked Milarepa to build a house for him. When it was finished, he asked him to tear it down and restore the stones and other materials used to their original places. Building and tearing down a second house, this time with a western aspect, followed; and later a third house with a northern aspect was partly built and demolished. Only a fourth one that Milarepa nearly completed was allowed to stay intact. Lāma Govinda in a separate work explains this house building venture as follows:

> His guru, Marpa, in order to make him expiate his former misdeeds and the bad karmic effects, which stood in the way of his spiritual progress, ordered him

to build with his own hands four houses and to destroy each of them after its completion, excepting the last. The ground-plan of the first house was circular, that of the second semi-circular or crescent-shaped, that of the third, triangular, and that of the fourth one square. In other words, Milarepa was made to concentrate upon the psychic centres of the elements, Water, Air, Fire, and Earth, which represent, as the text says, the four types of action, namely, the peaceful, the grand or far reaching, the powerful or fascinating, and the stern. He had thus to undo all his former actions by first reconstructing them and then dissolving them, right down to the foundation, the Muladhara, the element "Earth." Then only was he allowed to build the lasting edifice of his new spiritual life.[8]

While Milarepa was undergoing his trials and tribulations, Marpa is shown to be deliberately eccentric, arbitrary, short-tempered and once pretended to be drunk during a confrontation with the disciple. Milarepa scarcely had an occasion to get a glimpse or a sign of the guru's personal concern for him or sense some of the genuine human qualities of the guru. For the most part the probationary period is portrayed as being greatly a testing of the śiṣya's perseverance in learning to become physically, socially and spiritually independent, even under the most discouraging living circumstances. Marpa's wife is shown as being the opposite. Jetsün referred to her as "reverent mother" and while undergoing his harsh laboring trials she supplied him with chhang, and nicely cooked hot meals. When he was getting discouraged she would give him consolation and encouragement. The following example illustrates her supportive and encouraging role during a period after Milarepa had been struck and dragged out of the initiation circle by Marpa. While the disciple felt most dejected and seemed to be in a nearly hopeless state of mind, Marpa's wife went to him and said:

> The Lāma is beyond comprehension. He sayeth that he had brought the Sacred Doctrine from India into this land for the benefit of all sentient beings: and, as a rule, he will teach and preach to even a dog that may happen to come into his presence, and wind up by praying for its welfare. Still, do not lose faith in him.[9]

On various occasions she tried hard to be helpful when Milarepa was attempting to get initiated. She offered him some household belongings to be offered as initiation fees. When these were turned down by Marpa, she gave the disciple some of her own personal belongings; and when these were also turned down and confiscated as improperly held, undeclared items of her dowry, she resorted to cunning schemes. Finally, she decided that her husband would not initiate Jetsün so she is described as preparing and offering Marpa and his other disciples a brew of chhang that had a high alcoholic content. After they became intoxicated and fell asleep, she took from the lāma's room, among other things, Naropa's (Marpa's guru) garlands and rosary of rubies. She wrapped them in an expensive scarf, and produced a forged letter asking lāma Ngogdun-Chudor, a former disciple of Marpa, to accept the gifts and initiate and instruct the referred disciple. She convinced Milarepa to go ahead with that plan. Milarepa who had once before left Marpa for a few hours and returned on his own, went ahead with the plan. He was initiated and instructed, but made no progress; so in a fate-like fashion, he returned to his destined great guru to face the consequences of his transitional disbelief in the judgement and competence of the guru. Marpa at first displayed wrath and indignation. Subsequently, it appeared that without any further testing, the probationary period of the śiṣya was over. He was being initiated and the ceremony was held in his honor.

Attention should be given here to the symbolical significance placed on the disciple's attitude regarding sacrifice. In previous sections of the study, and particularly in the chapter on "The Guru-Disciple Relationship in the Bhagavad Gītā", it was brought out how important Jung considered the sacrificing of the ego to the Self in reference to the Individuation Process. Here in this Tāntrik Buddhist narrative can also be seen the emphasis placed on the conscious awareness of the nature of sacrificing. Milarepa was thrown out of the initiation circle on the grounds that he did not personally earn the fees he was offering for the great symbolic rite. What he was given as a casual gift was not considered as something consciously earned and deserving to be symbolically representing his sacrifice.

When Marpa asked his disciple Ngogdun-Chudor, who had offered him all his sheep and goats if there were any left, the latter indicated that there were none except a lame she-goat who couldn't make the journey. Marpa demanded that his senior disciple go back on his long journey home and bring that lame goat also. He previously had demanded that the same disciple return Naropa's garlands and rosary of rubies because he had received them under false premises. Yet, after the consecration ceremony was over, Marpa surprisingly told the same disciple that now he could have the garlands. It appears to this writer that conscious giving and accepting is stressed here. A total and consciously intended offering of the sheep and goats was so important that the inconvenience and apparent insignificance of bringing the lame goat should not interfere with the spirit of giving.

Following the ceremony, Marpa is presented explaining how he dealt with his role as Milarepa's guru and how he perceived the entire relationship situation between the disciple and himself. He is quoted as saying:

> When we come to think well over matters, no one seemeth to deserve blame. Wishing that Great Sorcerer (Jetsün) might be absolved from his sins, I caused him to build the edifices single-handed. Had it been for my selfish purpose, why I could have got on much better by coaxing and by gentle means than otherwise, hence, I was not to blame. As for Damema (his own wife), she being a woman and possessing a more than usual share of maternal sympathy and pity, could not bear to see me ill-treat poor Great Sorcerer, who seemed so willing, obedient, and patient. Who could blame her for furnishing him with the forged letter, and the accompanying tokens, although it was a rather serious thing to do? . . . As for thee Great Sorcerer, thou art quite right in trying to obtain Religious Truths by every possible means . . . I was deprived (meaning, Marpa, himself) of the chance of filling Great Sorcerer with despair, as I should have done. Therefore, was I angered; and, although my anger recoiled on me like a wave of water, yet it was not like a vulgar worldly anger. Religious anger is a thing apart; and, in whatever form it may appear, it hath the same object—to excite repentance and

thereby to contribute to the spiritual development of the person. . . . Had I had the chance of plunging this spiritual son of mine nine times into utter despair, he would have been cleansed thoroughly of all his sins. . . . That will not be so, and that he will still retain a small portion of his demerits, is due to Damema's ill-timed pity and narrow understanding . . . Now I am going to care for him and give him those Teachings and Initiations which I hold as dear as mine own heart. I, myself, will provide him with food while he is in retreat, and with mine own hands will enclose him in the place of meditation. Henceforth rejoice.[10]

It was indicated earlier that one of the main objectives in connection with the trials and tribulations that Milarepa underwent during his probationary period was the overcoming of handicapping dependency needs. These measures were designed to promote a sense of independence from physical and social influences that might interfere or distract from the demands of the Self-realization process. Pursuing this matter further, the text mentions that Marpa expressed anger in a religious sense to excite repentance. He actually tried to plunge his disciple into utter despair nine times and eight times he was able to do so. What is stressed is not merely the building of an attitude and behavioral habit pattern of great physical and psychological endurance. As it was already explained, using subtle motivational techniques with the disciple could accomplish this objective more effectively.

At a shallow face-value level, inducing repentance to expiate one's sins appears to be a simple intense emotional experience even when the intensity assumes the nature of deeply felt desperation. If one, however, examines seriously lāma Govinda's explanation regarding the meaning of Milarepa's building of the four houses, which was quoted earlier in this section, he will notice the deeper meaning of the state of repentance and desperation. Milarepa was made to concentrate upon the psychic centres of the four types of action. By doing this symbolically he would be reconstructing and then dissolving his actions down to the foundation at the lowest level, the Mūlādhāra, or Earth Element. That represented the undoing of his actions which was required before he could be allowed to build the lasting edifice of his spiritual life. This lasting edifice corresponds, in Analytical Psychology, to the building of an individuated personality.

The completion of the last edifice was also meant to correspond with the ending of the śisya's probationary testing period. Therefore, all the experiencing of desperation and repentance was to take place in connection with the feats of building, demolishing and reconstructing the edifice. Sinning in Buddhism is not just breaking socially imposed rules of conduct. The basic concern of Buddhism is that life is full of suffering. The four noble truths and the eight-fold path deal with the reality of such suffering and what can be possibly done about it.[11] It appears to this writer that in Buddhism, and particularly in regard to certain Mahāyāna teachings and practices, there is a great understanding of the psychological value of suffering. The more and deeper one suffers, the greater will tend to be his capacity to deal with the conditions connected with suffering. The value of suffering lies in its role of convincing the ego of its limitations and helplessness and the need for the ego to place itself in the service of the healing forces and wisdom of the Self. The quantity of suffering will not by itself convince the ego to surrender its misconceived sovereignty in favor of cooperating with the Self. Repenting to expiate one's sins, when considered at a deeper symbolic Buddhist level, implies that one accepts responsibility for the entire scope of his actions. Sinning, in this broader context, consists of the actions committed by the influence of the ego against the interests of the Self. Genuine repenting by inducement of suffering and despair involves a conscious awareness regarding the misguided activities of the ego and willingness on the part of the ego to submit to the Self and cooperate with it.

Upon completion of the probationary period, there was practically a reversal in the way the guru treated his śisya. Marpa now offered to personally supply his disciple with food and clothing and to instruct him with zeal in the highly treasured spiritual teachings. He displayed personal concern and warmth. He also showed confidence that the disciple could and would carry out the long-term, rigorous demands of spiritual attainment. Generally speaking, the guru was presented as a spiritual father who found it either essential or highly important to assume initially several of the features of the negative or terrible father. In reference to this Neumann says:

> . . .the divine father may easily be confused with the negative father, for the father who sends his son into danger is an ambiguous figure with personal and impersonal characteristics.[1][2]

Marpa was shown as having deliberately assumed the role of the terrible father and encouraged the disciple to overcome and kill symbolically the nature of such a father.[1][3] His subsequent attitude and behavior indicated that he also made great effort to generate and openly express a true spiritual father-son relationship. The relationship was aiming to assist the disciple to attain final victory and liberation. The initiations and teaching of the doctrines were only tools to help the sisya experience the higher truths. The guru was preparing the disciple to succeed him as one of the top leaders of the Kargyütpas, yet at no time did he make restrictive demands as a condition for this decision. Following his initiation by Marpa, Milarepa stayed with his guru at least one year and, as stated in the text, not more than a few years. Most of the time was spent in isolated meditation. Occasionally, he came out of his retreat and discussed his experiences with Marpa, and was given supplemental instruction.

An illustration was given showing the value of daring, deciding and acting which was contrary to the religious doctrinal rules. Milarepa, while on retreat, had a dream telling him, by means of a figure that appeared like a Dakini (fairy or goddess), that while he made much progress spiritually he still needed to master the teaching of the Drong-jug (a special yogic treatise), and he must procure it by all means. Milarepa, after reflecting on the dream, pulled down the stone and mud-built partition of his retreat enclosure and went to his guru. Marpa was shocked that the disciple would violate such a serious rule on meditative practices. After he listened, however, he accepted the judgement of the disciple as being a sensible one. He is even described going on a long and adventurous journey to India to find his own guru, Naropa, and procure from him the Drong-jug teaching for the benefit of his disciple and indirectly for other seekers who were to follow.

The guru is described as paying a great deal of attention to the individual needs of the disciples. The personal interests and temperaments of his śiṣyas were taken into consideration in determining particular methods and the scope of training. Out of several doctrinal teachings only certain ones were selected for studying, meditating and practicing purposes. In addition to using judgement based on personal contact and observation, Marpa is also reported to have relied on intuitive methods to find out which teaching resources were best suited to each of his principal four disciples.[14]

Guidance Through Dreams

When serious decisions were to be made or when some unusual event was to take place, both guru and śiṣyas seemed to rely heavily on the guiding value of dreams.

Rechung, one of Milarepa's advanced disciples, was inspired and guided by a dream to write the biography of his guru.[15] A review of the dream, which is given below, provides helpful hints regarding how it was interpreted.

Rechung dreamt that he was walking by the capital of the Urgyan land inhabited by male and female angels. It was a beautiful country and the houses and palaces in this city were built of gold, silver and precious stones. The inhabitants were physically attractive and wore beautiful silk garments and jewels. Among them he recognized an old acquaintance, a female disciple of one of his previous gurus in Nepal. She welcomed him by addressing him as 'nephew'; she took him to the center of the capital where the Akṣhobhya Buddha was sitting on a majestic throne preaching a sermon dealing with the lineage, birth and deeds of various Buddhas and Bodhisattvas. Finally he began to describe in detail the lives of the leading Kargyütpa gurus. In concluding his discourse, Akṣhobhya said that he would narrate the story of Jetsün Milarepa that would surpass in wonder the life history of the aforementioned beings. He invited those present to come and hear his presentation when it was going to be given.

Some of those present said that if this history is so interesting, it would be a sin if they, as disciples, did not hear it and by all means they should try to get the story told. When one asked, "Where is Milarepa now?" someone else replied that he was either in 'Og-min' (the Heaven of the Ādi-Buddha) or in 'Ngön-gah' (the Heaven of Indra or the Akṣhobhya-Buddha). Hearing these last remarks, Rechung thought, "Why Milarepa is now living in Tibet, but these people seem to be hinting that I should ask Milarepa, himself, to tell the story of his life; and that I will surely do." His fellow disciple companion then laid hold of his hand and shaking it joyfully she said, "Nephew, hast thou understood?" Rechung woke up with his mind feeling very clear and he also felt himself to be in a sincere, satisfying, devotional mood. He reflected on the dream and realized how fortunate he was to have known Milarepa in real life. Then it occured to him that he was showing stupidity by thinking in the dream that Milarepa was in Tibet when someone else was saying he was at 'Og-min' or 'Ngon-gah'. He interpreted the incident about the lady and those listening to the preaching, including the comments they made later, as being a divine injunction to write a biography of Jetsün.

Rechung fell asleep again and this time he saw five beautiful maidens, respectively white, blue, yellow, red, and green (these are Tāntrik Goddesses representing the five Incarnations of the Goddess Durga) come into his presence. One of them said, "Tomorrow the story of Milarepa is to be told; let us go and hear it!" A second one inquired, "Who is going to ask him to relate it?" A third maiden replied, "Jetsün's chief disciples are going to ask him." Meanwhile they were all glancing at Rechung smilingly. One of them made a final remark before they disappeared, "It behooveth the disciples to pray for the boon, and it shall be our duty and pleasure to spread and protect the Faith." Waking up, Rechung accepted this last phase of his dreaming as being a sign from the Immortal Sisters (referring to the five Dakinis or Goddesses). It reinforced his resolve from the previous dream to write the biography and to proceed by asking Milarepa to narrate his life history.

In dream interpretation, one of the basic premises, according to Jung, is to ask: What conscious attitude does the dream compensate? This necessitates that one relate the dream to the conscious situation. The conscious mind and the dream interact in the subtlest way. Jung considers the relationship between those two as being strictly causal.[16]

In Rechung's dream, what is stressed is the psychic symbolic level of the experience represented as an occurrence in a Buddhist state of Heaven. The dreamer experiences it as intensely and spiritually satisfying. At the same time, he becomes aware that his human guru has a most significant and honored place in this realm of his dreaming. After he woke up, he reflected and recognized that the dream pointed out that in his conscious attitude he had failed to appreciate the psychic depths and impact of his guru's personality. It appears to this writer that the dreamer in his interpretation is portrayed as having examined which conscious attitude his dream compensated, making it thus possible for the dream contents to be assimilated. He is shown as being aware of the intense impact of the dream and comparing the contents to his usual conscious attitudes. By attributing his exalting dream experience to a consequence of his Guru's Grace and contrasting this experience with his ordinary attitude toward the guru, and his spiritual attiude in general, he felt a need to modify his conscious attitude allowing the dream contents to be assimilated.

Rechung was also portrayed as having gotten the hint, through the first phase of his dreaming, to write the biography of his guru. The female figure that accompanied him in the dream was trying to make him understand something. The bystanders, referred to as disciples, had mentioned that they should pray and by all means try to get the life story told for the benefit of all beings. The dreamer is shown as looking for hints that would tie in adequately to his conscious situation. With such an approach, it can be easily understood why Rechung received encouragement through his dream to write the biography. The second dreaming phase makes the hints even more specific. The maidens are represented as the helpful forces or aspects of the anima (used in Jungian terms) encouraging him to take action. They are even looking at him, in the dream, as expecting that he truly get the message to go ahead and ask the guru to relate his life history. This part of the dream seems to be reinforcing the first one.

On the anniversary of his son's death, Marpa instructed his assembled disciples to observe their dreams after they retired, and report them to him later. He hoped that prophetic data would be revealed in the dreams regarding handling the succession and other matters of the Kargyütpa sect. Only Milarepa had a dream of prophetic significance; Marpa is shown as interpreting the dream in great detail. He does not use a semiotic interpretative approach. Special objects or incidents are viewed as symbols or symbolic events, in a manner resembling Jung's method of dealing with symbols. Jung states, "dream symbolism demands that we take into account the dreamer's philosophical, religious, and moral convictions." He also says:

> In theory relatively fixed symbols do exist whose meaning must on no account be referred to anything known and formulable as a concept. If there were no such relatively fixed symbols, it would be impossible to determine the structure of the unconscious, for there would be nothing that could in any way be laid hold of or described.[17]

Marpa seems to take into consideration the conscious status quo of the dreamer; he assumes that symbols are relatively fixed but that they are not signs and cannot be accurately conceptualized. Examination of a few incidents in the dream illustrate this point. For example, the concept of north does not have a fixed sign meaning. When used in the context of "Regions of the World's North" in which a grand mountain stood, north was interpreted as the country of Tibet, in accordance with the dreamer's background as a Tibetan and a Kargyütpa Buddhist. Tibet is located north of India which was the origin of Buddhism and in a sense a cultural-world center. Although Tibet is nothing but a mountainous country, the mountain is not taken to represent Tibet. To the devout Tibetan Buddhist, the mountain represented much more meaningfully his own religious sect. The mountain was touching the very skies. The goal of the Kargyütpas is to ascend from the roots of bodily-earthly existence, symbolized as the Mūlādhāra centre or stage, to the ethereal-transcendent, or Buddhahood state of being, symbolized as the centre or stage Sahasrāra. When "northward" of the mountain was mentioned later in the dream, this time north as a direction did not deal with a physical geographical location. Marpa relates this concept to the conscious background of the dreamer while still dealing with symbolical interpretation. The mountain represents the Kargyütpa sect, which is now the centre of attention; and there are four basic directions from the centre, as Marpa also had four chief disciples. Certain theriomorphic features and qualities are also described in connection with each of the four directions.

The interpreter now has sufficient hints to detect whether or not the qualities attributed to each animal or bird found in one of the four directions correspond to the qualities of the four chief disciples and how these relate to the concerns regarding the future of the Kargyütpa sect. All four—the lion, the tigress, the eagle, and the vulture—look heavenward, which represents the highest goal of the Kargyütpas. The appearance and features of the animals and birds and the nature of their activity supply several clues regarding the role of the four disciples in connection with the future of their religious organization.

These dreams, whether actually dreamt or just portrayed as dreams, are rich in symbolism and convincingly indicate that Tāntrik Buddhists had some insightful knowledge on how to interpret dreams. From the standpoint of Analytical Psychology, when interpreting dreams, attention must be given to the conscious situation of the dreamer and the conscious attitude which the dream compensates in order to facilitate the process of assimilating unconscious contents. Regarding the interpretation of the dreams mentioned in the biography of Milarepa, there are sufficient indications that all these factors were to some extent applied sensibly. The examples showed how attention was paid to the conscious outlook and background of the dreamer and what conscious attitude the dream compensated. Regarding deeper knowledge of folklore and mythology for a better understanding of the symbolical archetypal aspects of dreams, the Tāntrik Buddhist gurus and disciples had not an extensive, but intensive and specilized background. They were well-informed regarding Hindu and Tibetan folklore, mythology and legendary works. Their training along these lines supplied them with valuable insight in regard to the symbolical nature of unconscious contents. They did not, however, have what would be considered a broad background in comparative mythology and folklore as defined by analytical psychologists.

Jung, in his commentary on The *Tibetan Book of the Great Liberation,* which is a Tāntrik Buddhist text, stated that the East bases itself on psychic reality. In addition to the many advantages that exist in such a psychological introverted approach, he pointed out how the East, and particularly here the Kargyütpa approach, depreciates the extraverted, object-oriented approach as an illusory desirousness, as existence in the Saṃsāra and the source of all suffering.[18] This over-emphasis may interfere with the process of consciously assimilating unconscious contents.

On the other hand, there are certain safeguards to offset the appeal of the extreme ascetic ideal of overcoming existence in the Saṃsāra. The ultimate premise of Tantrik Buddhism is that the Saṃsāra and Nirvana are One. Realization of this becomes the main challenge and not necessarily negation or rejection of earthly existence. Extreme asceticism is only one way of attaining the Highest Realization.

It should be noted that, according to Kargyütpa teachings, dreaming is considered to be an active means in the attainment of enlightenment. The place where dreams originate is the total man, the stirring of motility in the primordial radiant light.[19] For this reason dreams are considered so important. They facilitate communication with the Collective Unconscious, or the Universal Mind of the Buddhist Tāntriks. Milarepa had remained at his guru's for a period of a few years, but only during the end of his stay did he receive his last and highest initiations and the mysteries of the Dream Symbols.[20]

In addition to the views and practices regarding dreams that were already mentioned, the Tāntrik Buddhists often try to develop the skill of being aware during dreaming, while one is not awake but actually in the dreaming state. The purpose of such a practice is to develop discrimination and ability to differentiate among different states of being.[21]

Examining the various dreams mentioned in Milarepa's biography, one often notices that the dreamer does not hastily assign arbitrary interpretations to his dream. He usually seeks, through reflection on his conscious situation, or through other related dreams, corroborative evidence for his tentative interpretive conclusions. For instance, Rechung, after his second dream, was much more sure regarding the meaning of the first and the second combined. Marpa, just before Milarepa arrived at his home, felt definitely more assured regarding the clues of his dream when he listened to the relevant elements in his wife's dream. When Marpa was hoping to receive dream guidance regarding the future of his religious order, he asked all four of his chief disciples to observe and report their dreams. He wanted to compare them for corroborative interpretation purposes, although at the end one dream only seemed to contain any pertinent information. Jung, on many occasions, stressed how important it is to look at a series of dreams, or at any other corroborative evidence that will bring out meaning and purpose to the dreamer's situation. In reference to the latter part of the last statement, Jung made the following remarks:

> I know that if we meditate on a dream sufficiently long and thoroughly, if we carry it around with us and turn it over and over, something almost always comes of it. This something is not, of course, a scientific result to be boasted about or rationalized; but it is an important practical hint which shows the patient what the unconscious is aiming at. . .I must content myself wholly with the fact that the result means something to the patient and sets his life in motion again. I may allow myself only one criterion for the result of my labours: Does it work? As for my scientific hobby—my desire to know why it works--this I must reserve for my spare time.[22]

In this sense it can be safely said that the Kargyütpas did look at their dreams seriously; they did turn them over and over and carried them with them and did many more things with their dreams than many patients in analysis, but not necessarily any more or as much as patients embarking upon the Individuation Process.

Psychological Implications

Earlier in this chapter, it was shown how Milarepa accepted the heroic call and started on his Self-realization journey. In that period, he became aware of the conflicting forces inside and around him. People did not accept him any longer as a nice innocent and mistreated lad. Thus he was induced to discontinue wearing the mask of innocence and deal with the problems associated with the persona. His guilt, and fear of after-death punishment for the destructive and murderous deeds that he committed, portray him as becoming aware of the shadow aspects of his nature. Later, during the probationary period, as a disciple of Marpa, Jetsün had to struggle quite intensely to work out problems in the areas of what Jung called the personal unconscious.

In dealing with the anima, which is at a somewhat deeper level, bordering the Collective Unconscious, Milarepa's situation and reactions were more complicated to interpret. Jetsün was presented as having had a positive relationship with his personal mother, with the wife of his guru of the black arts, with Damema, who was the wife of his chief guru, Marpa, and with feminine figures of his dreams. As a matter of fact, in some ways the relationship was too good for his own best interests. In this way he appeared receptive and subject to many constructive and helpful influences of the anima. Not having developed yet an adequate conscious discriminating function, he allowed the anima to operate as an autonomous complex exerting, at times, its negative and terrible aspects.[23] In a sense it could be stated that a deep connection with the anima often contains a need for an unreserved trusting of the feminine principle. As explained above and elsewhere, this can be a great asset in some respects and quite a liability in others. The dual effects produced by the anima were indicated in the relationship of Milarepa with his own mother. In many ways she cared for him, and in other ways she influenced him to carry out behavior that was destructive to both of them. Yet considered from a different standpoint, it was the painful consequence of the mother-instigated behavior that set Jetsün on his journey. Another incident demonstrating how the positively intended influence of the anima actually resulted in a setback in Self-development for Milarepa was Damema's scheming during the probationary period. This incident was related in a previous section of this chapter. At the same time, however, Damema did help Jetsün in many constructive ways. She constantly gave him moral support and took care of his material needs at a time when he desperately needed help. Without her support, it would have been practically impossible to complete the probationary period trials.

The helpful aspect of the anima was shown again at a later time. His sister, Peta, and Zesay, a childhood bride and companion who according to family tradition would have also been his adulthood bride consummating the marriage, had Milarepa not chosen to lead a chaste, ascetic life, visited him several times and supplied him with provisions while he was meditating in caverns and in an extremely deteriorated state of health caused by malnutrition. This time, however, he dealt with the feminine in a different manner. He accepted the nourishing food that his body needed so desperately, but he did not yield to the pleadings of his sister to give up his ascetic life and beg alms for his sustenance. Neither was he moved by her argument that nearly all lāmas in the course of exercising their duties were making sufficient income to live comfortable lives.

Regarding Milarepa's reactions to the provided nourishment and general helpfulness of the anima in the persons of his sister and Zesay, he was quoted as saying:

> The knowledge I now have obtained was born of my previous energetic devotions, which had served as its main cause; and it only awaited the accident, at the crisis, of the wholesome and nourishing food, and the timely prescription contained in the scroll, to bring it forth. My belief in the methods of the Mantrayānic doctrines, which teach that a real transcendent knowledge can be obtained by proper care of the body and without giving up nourishing food and comfortable clothing, was established. I also saw that Peta and Zesay

had greatly contributed to the final development of the hitherto latent qualities, and therefore mine obligation to them was great.[24]

Milarepa at this stage seems to have accepted the cooperative nourishing and sustaining role of the anima without allowing her, any longer, a domineering autonomous-complex status. He has now reached the point of consciously assuming responsibility for his decisions. He is partly successful in convincing his sister to accept the teachings of Buddhism. His paternal aunt, who comes to him with a repentful attitude, was, through his influence, converted to a genuine religious way of life.

Milarepa's confrontation with the anima took place over a long period of time, but the real impact of dealing with it was shown mainly in the incident describing the events involving Peta and Zesay which were mentioned above. Immediately following his reactions to that occurrence, Jetsün related the following event which seemed to have a great effect on him:

> I experienced a state of supersensual calmness and clearness resembling the former states which I had experienced, but exceeding them in its depth and ecstatic intensity, and therein differing from them. Thus was a hitherto unknown and transcendent knowledge born in me. . .[25]

For the first time in his life he seemed to have made a connection with the masculine spirit in a way that enabled him to bring out his own spirit vigorously and impressively. It was at this time that people first noticed something special when he gave sermons and sang devotional songs. On previous occasions they had only noticed that he had a beautiful singing voice or that he was a promising devotee, but now they began to sense his emerging masculine spirit. The timing of this experience, in reference to the sequence of Milarepa's psychological development, seems to correspond to the Analytical Psychological stage that deals with the archetype of the Old Wise Man. In reference to this point, Jacobi made the following comments:

So it is no accident that after the confrontation with the soul-image the appearance of the archetype of the Old Wise Man, the personification of the spiritual principle, can be distinguished as the next milestone of inner development.[26]

After establishing his relationship with the spirit, Milarepa was shown dealing with the problem of inflation. Throughout his stay at Marpa's, and up to this time, Jetsün did not display any personal possession of supernormal powers. His previous involvement in sorcery was described as an incidental and unusual skill, but not as something that made him feel that he was the possessor of supernatural powers. In this stage Milarepa had several encounters with the mana personality archetype.[27] The quotations below describe how he reacted to some of these experiences and how he eventually dealt with his inflationary tendencies and the over-all archetypal problem:

I began to feel that I had obtained the power of transforming myself into any shape (desired), and of flying through the air. By day, I thus felt that I could exercise endless phenomenal powers; by night, in my dreams, I could traverse the universe in every direction unimpededly--from the summit of Mount Meru (The Great Central Mountain of Buddhist and Hindu mythology, round which the cosmos is disposed in seven concentric circles of intervening seas and mountains) to its base--and I saw everything clearly. Likewise (in my dreams) I could multiply myself into hundreds of personalities, all endued with the same powers as myself. Each of my multiplied forms could traverse space and go to some Buddha Heaven, listen to the Teachings there, and then come back and preach the Dharma to many persons. I could also transform my physical body into a blazing mass of fire, or into an expanse of flowing or calm water. . .finally, I actually could fly . . . now, that I had obtained transcendent knowledge and siddhi (super-normal powers), and had been seen flying by human beings, if I continued here, worldly folk would flock to me, praying for protection from harm and the fulfillment of selfish desires. This would be courting the temptations of the Son of the Celestials. Worldly fame and prosperity might retard the progress of my devotion and obscure my spiritual knowledge: so I resolved to go and carry on my meditation in the solitudes of Lapchi-Chūbar.[28]

These experiences, whether they are considered literally or symbolically (and examining them in terms of the latter has been the present objective) do show inflationary involvement and a decision to deal with the inflation. By sacrificing worldly fame and other forms of ego glorification, Milarepa sacrificed the ego to a higher principle.

Immediately following the period of dealing with inflation, Milarepa was described as being well advanced along the Nirvānic Path. He still spent long periods of meditation in various caves dealing with the final major confrontation challenge, which was the archetype of the Self. Only at that point his role as a guru was brought out dramatically. His fate as a hero was re-emphasized by giving him supernatural attributes and ending in a state of triumphal apotheosis. In Analytical Psychology the theme of the hero's triumphal apotheosis symbolizes the completion of the goal which is the journey of the hero or the Self-realization process.

Chapter VII

SUMMARY

The optimum communication, relatedness and union between the Divine Guru and the finite disciple was the major goal of Eastern spiritual disciplines. It was indicated repeatedly in the Gītā, for example, that man should accept his totality; the human ego with its activities should not be renounced, but man, through his entire conscious efforts, should place his activities into the service of the Supreme Self. One should only renounce the desire and fruits of action, but not action itself. All activities should be offered as sacrifice to the Divine.

According to Jung, the act of making a sacrifice consists in giving something which belongs to oneself. If it is to be a true sacrifice, the gift must be given as if it were being destroyed. Genuine sacrifice involves a conscious and deliberate self-surrender. This intentional loss is also a gain, for if one can give himself it proves that he possesses himself.

Referring to the Self-realization process, the acts of consecration, sacrifice and surrender of the ego to the Self must be carried on continually. Therefore, any relationship between a disciple and the guru, whether it be the Supreme or the human guru, must take into serious account the on-going nature and expression of sacrifice. The same would apply in the case of any relationship between the analysand and the Unconscious or between the analysand and the analyst.

In Analytical Psychology, psychotherapy is a dialectic relationship between psychotherapist and patient. It is a prolonged dialogue between two psychic entities. Knowledge is used only as a tool. The real purpose is transformation, involving an indeterminable change which eventually eliminates the rule of the ego. The psychotherapist cannot provoke the transformation experience. He can only help the patient to develop an attitude which opposes minimum resistance to the decisive experience.

According to Jung, the therapeutic effect of the analytic method is derived from the psychotherapist's efforts to enter the psyche of the patient and to establish a psychologically adapted relationship. The transference, with all its projected content, is the patient's attempt to get into psychological rapport with the psychotherapist. He needs such a relationship in order to overcome the disassociated state. The transference consists of a number of projections which act as a substitute for a real psychological relationship. The patient turns to the psychotherapist as an object of purely human relationship in which each individual is guaranteed his proper place. Only when the projections are recognized as such, is the particular form of rapport known as the transference at an end, and then the problem of individual relationship begins. This kind of personal relationship is a freely negotiated bond where the patient confronts the psychotherapist with the same kind of ruthless criticism that he learns from the therapist in the course of the treatment and over-all psychic development. In this dialectic relationship both patient and psychotherapist are equally involved.

The main purpose of the human guru-disciple relationship is transformation which, as in Analytical Psychology, eventually eliminates the rule of the ego. The guru basically recognizes that he cannot force upon the disciple a change that will produce Liberation or Enlightenment. Through the initiatory, instructional and other aspects of the relationship he can only help the disciple to develop an attitude that will offer the least resistance to the essential experience.

In some Eastern systems there is much more opportunity for a dialectic relationship between the guru and the disciple than there is in others. Often during the initial stages, the relationship is kept at a formal level and there is very little personal contact between the disciple and the guru. During later stages, the relation tends to be more informal and cordial. Even during certain advanced stages, the contact with the guru may be infrequent if the disciple is required to engage in meditative or other isolating practices over long periods of time. The relationship between Milarepa and his guru, Marpa, serves as a typical illustration of the points just made.

Despite intermittent restrictions regarding the frequency of seeing each other, there is often a deep human bond between the disciple and the guru. Cultural factors may affect the outer expression of this most meaningful relationship. Essentially, however, this experience resembles what Jung called the real human relationship which is established at the more advanced stages of analysis, after the basic transference problem has been resolved.

Generally speaking, the disciple is expected to treat his guru with great respect, confidence and devotion. The customary ways of paying great tribute to the guru and submitting to his authority do not necessarily interfere with the cultivation of a genuine human relationship. It appears to this writer that the less a guru and/or a disciple is psychically developed the more dependent and asymmetrical their relationship will tend to be and the reverse would also be applicable. The guru accepts the outward authority granted to his role, but in a deeper sense he often expresses and communicates a sense of humility, human concern and reciprocity toward the disciple. Doctrinal factors affect to some extent the nature and depth of the relationship.

Although the relationship of the Divine Guru and his disciple in the Gītā was mostly symbolical, it nevertheless pointed out the kinship that existed between the two. The dialectic element of the relation was clearly brought out; yet Kṛṣṇa, by the very means of the dialogue, convinced his disciple of the need to accept the full authority of the guru and with unreserved devotion place himself in the service of his Master. For the same purpose and in the same spirit, the human guru has been accorded with such devotion and respect in the Vedas, Upaniṣads, Tantras, Purāṇas and Buddhist writings.

Following the probationary period, Milarepa's relationship with his guru was a deeply meaningful and cordial one. At times they both exchanged notes regarding the disciple's experiences in connection with his psychic development. Marpa paid much attention to the individual needs, temperament and talents of his disciples and dealt with them accordingly. There were apparently some elements of a dialectic relationship between Marpa and his disciples, but a full dialogue did not take place between them.

Ramakrishna encouraged and promoted a sense of kinship between his disciples and himself. He allowed some of his disciples to confront and challenge him on various occasions. He even encouraged lay devotees to become involved in a dialogue with him. He did not hesitate to admit his human shortcomings, and he confronted others daringly, relying on his psychic and spiritual insights. More than many great gurus, he paid attention to individual needs, talents and the personality makeup of his disciples.

Sri Aurobindo eloquently explained how the human guru should, figuratively speaking, deal with the disciple as much as possible as the Supreme Guru deals with man. He pointed out that instruction is of some value, but the living example of the guru is more effective, particularly the example and overall impact of his inner realization.

Accepting and dealing with the individual differences and uniqueness of each disciple was, perhaps, stressed more by Sri Aurobindo than any other renowned Eastern guru. According to him, the Divine as a Principle or Essence is involved in the process of uniting with the finite nature of man to produce an evolutionary transformation. This is a symmetrical type of relationship between the Divine or Self and ego-conscious man. In this context the Divine is the Supreme Guru and man is his disciple. The guru is only a medium to assist the disciple to become a disciple of the Supreme Guru. In a parallel course, the Jungian analyst, while using different methods, attempts to assist the analysand to establish a relationship with the Collective Unconscious which will eventually be permanent and will require no further help from the analyst.

FOOTNOTES

Chapter I.

[1] M. Eliade, *Yoga: Immortality and Freedom* (New York: Pantheon Books, 1958). p. 12.

[2] Ibid., p. 11.

[3] S. Radhakrishnan, *The Principal Unpanisads* (London: George Allen & Unwin Ltd., 1953), p. 49.

[4] Ibid., pp.52-3.

[5] Ibid., p.77.

[6] S. Chatterjee & D. Datta, *An Introduction to Indian Philosophy* (Calcutta: Calcutta University Press, 1960), pp. 133-39.

[7] A. Coomaraswami, *Hinduism & Buddhism* (New York: Philosophical Library), p. 45 and pp. 62-7.

[8] S. Dasgupta, *Introduction to Tāntric Buddhism* (Calcutta: University of Calcutta, 1958), pp. 29-33.

[9] Badarayana, *Brahma Sutra* (London: George Allen & Unwin Ltd., 1960), pp. 207-23.

[10] M. Eliade, *Birth & Rebirth, The Religious Meaning of Initiation in Human Culture* (New York: Harper & Co., 1958).

[11] M. Eliade, *Yoga: Immortality and Freedom* op. cit., pp. 99-100.

[12] C.G. Jung, *Aion*, Vol. 9, Part II of *The Collected Works* (New York: Pantheon Books, 1959), p. 268.

[13] Ibid., pp. 223-32.

[14] C.G. Jung, *Two Essays on Analytical Psychology*, Vol. 7 of *The Collected Works* (London: Routledge & Kegan Paul, 1953), pp. 237-38.

[15] Ibid., p. 175.

[16] E. Harding, *Psychic Energy: Its Source and Goal* (New York: Pantheon Books, 1948), pp. 313, 316, 365, 410 and 337-38.

[17] C.G. Jung, *The Practice of Psychotherapy*, Vol. 16 of *The Collected Works* (New York: Pantheon Books, 1954), p. 102.

[18] C.G. Jung, *Psychology and Religion*, Vol. 11 of *The Collected Works* (New York: Pantheon Books, 1958), pp. 197-98.

[19] Ibid., p. 263.

[20] Ibid., pp. 467-68.

[21] Harding, op. cit., pp. 296-355.

Chapter II.

[1] A. Avalon, *Principles of Tantra* (Madras: Ganesh & Co., 3rd ed., 1960), p. 535.

[2] Ibid., p. 536.

[3] Ibid., p. 534.

[4] Ibid., p. 531.

[5] Ibid., pp. 46-52.

[6] Ibid., pp. 538-39.

[7] Ibid., pp. 543-44.

[8] Ibid., pp. 539-41.

[9] Ibid., pp. 545-48.

[10] Ibid., pp. 548-49.

[11] Ibid., p. 548.

[12] Ibid., pp. 569-70.

[13] Ibid., pp. 583-84.

[14] Ibid., pp. 579-81.

[15] M. Fordham, (ed.) "Symposium on Training", Vol. 6, No. 2 of *Journal of Analytical Psychology,* (July, 1961), p.95.

[16] M. Fordham, *New Developments in Analytical Psychology* (London: Routledge & Kegan Paul, 1957), p. 68.

[17] A. Avalon, op. cit., pp. 555-81.

[18] C.G. Jung, *Psychology & Religion* (New York: Pantheon Books, 1963), p. 554.

[19] C.G. Jung, *The Practice of Psychotherapy* (New York: Pantheon Books, 1954), pp. 96-100.

Chapter III.

[1] H. Chatterji, *The Bhagavad Gita* (New York: The Julian Press, Inc., 1960), pp. 2-3.

[2] A. Ghose, *Essays on the Gita* (Calcutta: Arya Publishing House, 1916), p. 15.

[3] Ibid., pp. 14-23.

[4] Ibid., p. 25.

[5] Ibid., p. 52.

[6] A. Ghose, *The Synthesis of Yoga* (New York: The Sri Aurobindo Library, Inc., 1950), pp. 65-68.

[7] C.G. Jung, *Psychology and Religion,* Vol. 11 of *The Collected Works* (New York: Pantheon Books, 1958), pp. 254-58.

[8] Ibid., p. 262.

Chapter IV.

[1] A. Ghose, *The Synthesis of Yoga* (New York: The Sru Aurobindo Library, Inc., 1950), p. 14.

[2] Ibid., p. 16.

[3] Ibid., pp. 10-11.

[4] Ibid., p. 1.

[5] A. Ghose, *Essays on the Gita* (Calcutta: Arya Publishing House, 1916), pp. 183-84.

[6] A. Ghose, *The Synthesis of Yoga,* op. cit., p. 2.

[7] Ibid., pp. 21-22.

[8] Ibid., pp. 20-27.

[9] Ibid., p. 11.

[10] Ibid., p. 17.

[11] Ibid., pp. 18-19.

[12] C.G. Jung, *The Practice of Psychotherapy,* Vol. 16 of *The Collected Works* (New York: Pantheon Books, 1954), p. 311.

[13] C.G. Jung & C. Kerenyi, *Essays on a Science of Mythology* (New York: Pantheon Books, 1949).

[14] C.G. Jung, *Psychology and Religion,* Vol. 11 of *The Collected Works* (New York: Pantheon Books, 1958), pp. 485, 502 and 510.

[15] C.G. Jung, *The Practice of Psychotherapy,* op. cit., pp. 183 and 248.

[16] J. Jacobi, (ed.), *Psychological Reflections* (New York: Pantheon Books, 1953), pp. 76-80.

[17] Ibid., p. 72.

[18] Ibid., p. 80.

Chapter V.

[1] Swami Nikhilananda, *The Gospel of Sri Ramakrishna* (New York: Ramakrishna-Vivekananda Center, 1942), p. 5.

[2] Ibid., pp. 12-13.

[3] Ibid., pp. 13-14.

[4] Ibid., p. 15.

[5] Ibid., p. 16.

[6] C. Isherwood, *Ramakrishna and His Disciples* (New York: Simon & Schuster, 1965), p. 70.

[7] Swami Nikhilananda, op. cit., pp. 18-19.

[8] Ibid., pp. 20-22.

[9] Ibid., p. 23.

[10] Ibid., p. 29.

[11] C.G. Jung, *Civilization in Transition*, Vol. 10 of *The Collected Works* (New York: Pantheon Books, 1964), p. 123.

[12] Swami Saradananda, *Sri Ramakrishna the Great Master* (Madras: Sri Ramakrishna Math, 1952). pp. 65-67.

[13] Ibid., pp. 240-243.

[14] Nikhilananda, op. cit., p. 184.

[15] C.G. Jung, *The Archetypes of the Collective Unconscious*, Vol. 9 of *The Collected Works* (New York: Pantheon Books, 1959), pp. 86-87.

[16] C.G. Jung, *The Practice of Psychotherapy*, Vol. 16 of *The Collected Works* (New York: Pantheon Books, 1954), pp. 173-74.

[17] Swami Saradananda, op. cit., pp. 56-57.

[18] C.G. Jung, *Memories, Dreams, Reflections* (New York: Pantheon Books, 1961), pp. 182-83.

[19] C.G. Jung, *Two Essays in Analytical Psychology*, Vol. 7 of *The Collected works* (London: Routledge & Kegan Paul, Ltd., 1953), pp. 140 & 167-69.

[20] Swami Nikhilananda, op. cit., p. 640.

[21] Ibid.

[22] Swami Saradananda, op. cit., pp. 79-80.

[23] Swami Nikhilananda, op. cit., pp. 141-42.

[24] C.G. Jung, *The Practice of Psychotherapy*, op. cit., pp. 72-73.

[25] Ibid., p. 75.

[26] Swami Saradananda, op. cit., pp. 606-07.

[27] Swami Nikhilananda, op. cit., p. 83.

[28] H. Chaudhuri, *Integral Yoga* (London: George Allen & Unwin Ltd., 1965), pp. 72-74.

[29] C.G. Jung, *Psychology and Religion* Vol. 11 of *The Collected Works* (New York: Pantheon Books, 1963), pp. 379-493.

[30] Swami Nikhilananda, op. cit., p. 150.

[31] Ibid., p. 140.

[32] Swami Saradananda, op. cit., p. 229.

[33] C.G. Jung, *The Practice of Psychotherapy*, op. cit., pp. 45-46.

[34] Ibid., pp. 48-50.

[35] Swami Saradananda, op. cit., pp. 162-67.

[36] C.G. Jung, *Psychology and Religion*, op. cit., pp. 386-97.

[37] Swami Nikhilananda, op. cit., pp. 137-39.

[38] C. Isherwood, op. cit., pp. 247-56.

[39] Swami Nikhilananda, op. cit., p. 125.

[40] C.G. Jung, *Psychology and Religion*, op. cit., pp. 483-84.

Chapter VI.

[1] W.Y. Evans-Wentz, *Tibet's Great Yogi Milarepa* (London: Oxford University Press, 1951 ed. and 1963 3rd Impression), pp. 1-29.

[2] Esther Harding, *Journey Into Self* (New York: Longmans, Green & Co., 1956), p. 4.

[3] E. Neumann, *The Origins and History of Consciousness* (New York: Pantheon Books, 1954), pp. 152-53, 195-219 and 397-418.

[4] Evans-Wentz, op. cit., p. 87.

[5] Ibid., p. 87.

[6] Ibid., pp. 88-89.

[7] Lama A. Govinda, *Foundations of Tibetan Mysticism* (New York: E.P. Dutton & Co., Inc., 1960), pp. 178-80.

[8] Ibid., p. 186.

[9] Evans-Wentz, op. cit., pp. 102-3.

[10] Ibid., pp. 130-31.

[11] S. Chatterjee & D. Datta, *An Introduction to Indian Philosophy* (Calcutta: University of Calcutta Press, 1960), pp. 115-133.

[12] Neumann, op. cit., 177.

[13] Ibid., pp. 170-91.

[14] Evans-Wentz, op. cit., pp. 154-55.

[15] Ibid., pp. 41-43.

[16] C.G. Jung, *The Practice of Psychotherapy*, Vol. 16 of *The Collected Works* (New York: Pantheon Books, 1954), pp. 151-57.

[17] Ibid., p. 156.

[18] C.G. Jung, *Psychology & Religion*, Vol. 11 of *The Collected Works* (New York: Pantheon Books, 1963), p. 481.

[19] H.V. Guenther, *The Life and Teaching of Naropa* (Oxford: Clarendon Press, 1963), p. 183.

[20] Evans-Wentz, op., City., p. 160.

[21] Guenther, op. cit., pp. 187-88.

[22] C.G. Jung, *The Practice of Psychotherapy*, op. cit., pp. 42-43.

[23] C.G. Jung, *Two Essays on Analytical Psychology* (London: Routledge & Kegan Paul, 1953), pp. 186-204.

[24] Evans-Wentz, op. cit., p. 209.

[25] Ibid., p. 208.

[26] J. Jacobi, *The Psychology of C. G. Jung* (New Haven: Yale University Press, 1951), p. 164.

[27] C.G. Jung, *Two Essays in Analytical Psychology*, op. cit., pp. 225-29.

[28] Evans-Wentz, op. cit., pp. 211-13.

DEFINITION OF TERMS

1. Analytical Psychological Terms[1]

Archetypes: They are the separate elements that make up the Collective Unconscious. They are invisible patterns of psychological functioning, of apperception, feeling, cognition, that operate when some life situation stimulates them in the unconscious. They correspond to the instincts in the physiological realm and, when activated, determine the form of experience. They are embedded in the unconscious and can only be deduced from their effects. They manifest themselves in symbols (Jung's definition of symbol).

Assimilation: It is the absorption or joining up of a new conscious content to already prepared subjective material, whereby the similarity of the new content with the waiting subjective material is specially emphasized, even to the prejudice of the independent quality of the new content. Fundamentally, assimilation is a process of apperception, which, however, is distinguished from pure apperception by this element of adjustment to the subjective material. This concept is employed in a broad sense as the adjustment of object to subject in general.

Collective: All those psychic contents Jung terms Collective which are peculiar not to one individual, but to many, at the same time, i.e. either to a society, a people, or to mankind in general. Such contents are the "mystical collective ideas" of the primitive described by Levy-Bruhl; they also include the general concepts of right, the State, religion, science, etc., current among civilized man. Feelings are termed collective.

Compensation: It means a balancing or supplementing. Jung conceives this term as a general functional adjustment, an inherent self regulation of the psychic apparatus. In this sense, he regards the activity of the unconscious (q.v.) as a compensation to the onesidedness of the general attitude produced by the function of consciousness.

Complexes: They are ideas, affectively toned, which tend to become associated around certain basic nuclei. The nucleus is a kind of psychological magnet with energic value, and automatically attracts ideas to itself in proportion to its energy. A complex may be partly or fully conscious or unconscious.

Consciousness: By Consciousness, Jung understands the relatedness of psychic contents to the ego insofar as they are sensed as such by the ego. Consciousness is the function or activity which maintains the relation of psychic contents with the ego.

Differentiation: It means the development of differences, the separation of parts from a whole. In reference to Jung's work on psychological types, the term is employed chiefly in respect to psychological functions.

110

Ego: It is defined as a complex of representations which constitutes the centrum of one's field of consciousness and appears to possess a very high degree of continuity and identity.

Extraversion: It means an outward-turning of the libido. With this concept Jung denotes a manifest relatedness of subject to object in the sense of a positive movement of subjective interest towards the object.

Feeling: It is defined as one of the four basic psychological functions. It is primarily a process that takes place between the ego and a given content, a process, that imparts to them definite value in the sense of acceptance or rejection. Feeling is an entirely subjective process, which may be in every respect independent of external stimuli, although chiming in with every sensation. Feeling is an independent function but under certain conditions it may lapse into a state of dependence upon another function, such as thinking.

Function: Psychological function is defined as a certain form of psychic activity that remains theoretically the same under varying circumstances. From the energic standpoint a function is a phenomenal form of libido (q.v.) which theoretically remains constant, in much the same way as physical force can be considered as the form of momentary manifestation of physical energy. Jung distinguishes four basic functions in all, two rational and two irrational--viz. thinking and feeling, sensation and intuition. These functions are differentiated from one another because they are neither mutually relatable nor mutually reducible.

Individuality: By individuality Jung understands the peculiarity and singularity of the individual in every psychological respect. Everything is individual that is not collective; everything, in fact, that pertains only to one and not to a larger group of individuals.

Individuation: It is the process of forming and specializing the individual nature; in particular, it is the development of the psychological individual as a differentiated being from the general, collective psychology. Individuation, therefore, is a process of differentiation, having for its goal the development of the individual personality. This concept is treated in detail in Chapter II of this study.

Introversion: It means a turning inwards of the libido (q.v.) whereby a negative relation of subject to object is expressed. Interest does not move towards the object, but recedes towards the subject.

Intuition: According to Jung, it is a basic psychological function. It transmits perceptions in an unconscious way. Everything, whether outer or inner objects or their associations, can be the object of this perception.

Libido: According to Jung this concept is synonymous with psychic energy. Psychic energy is the intensity of the psychic process--its psychological value. Frequently this term is used in a broad sense to denote energy.

Persona: It is a complicated system of relations between individual consciousness and society, fittingly enough a kind of mask, designed on the one hand to make a definite impression upon others, and, on the other, to conceal the true nature of the individual.

Projection: It signifies the transveying of a subjective process in an object. It is a process of dissimilation wherein a subjective content is estranged from the subject and, in a sense, incorporated in the object.

Self: This concept is elaborately explained in Chapter II of this study.

Sensation: It is the psychological function that mediates the perception of a physical stimulus. It is, therefore, identical with perception.

Shadow: It is designated as the negative side of the personality, the sum of all those unpleasant qualities that humans like to hide, together with the contents of the personal unconscious.

Soul (anima): By soul Jung means a definitely demarcated function-complex that is best characterized as a 'personality.'

Thinking: It is one of the four basic psychological functions. It is the function which, following its own laws, brings the contents of ideation into conceptual connection with one another.

Type: In a broad sense a type is a specimen, or example, which reproduces in a characteristic way the character of a species or general class. In reference to Jung's work on 'Psychological Types' a type is a characteristic model of a general attitude (q.v.) occurring in many individual forms.

Unconscious: It is defined here as an exclusively psychological and not a philosophical concept. It is a psychological boundary-concept, which covers all those psychic contents of processes which are not conscious, i.e. not related to the ego in a perceptible way.

2. Sanskrit Terms Used[2]

Avatār(a): A rare person in history whose soul or mind is not in process of evolution or re-incarnation, but is specially formed by a descent into humanity from the divine realm alone; an incarnation of God.

Avidyā: Ignorance or error. Fundamentally the mistake of regarding the temporary as eternal and the not-self as self.

Bhagavad Gītā: The well known Hindu scripture which is often referred to as The Song of God.

Bhagavata: The sacred book of the Hindus, especially of the Vaishnavas, dealing with the life of Sri Kṛṣṇa.

Bhairava: An aspirant of the Tāntrik sect; also denotes the God Śiva, especially in his frightful forms.

Bhakti: Devotion to God or love of God; single-minded devotion to one's Chosen Ideal.

Brahmā: The aspect of the Divine unity of God whose undertaking is creation.

Brahman or Brahmā: The one absolute being; also pure consciousness and undiluted joy or bliss; the one self of all and union with which is the goal of Vedanta.

Brāhmin: The highest caste in Hindu society.

Buddha: One who is enlightened; the founder of Buddhism.

Buddhi: The intelligence or discrimination faculty.

Chaitanya: Spiritual Consciousness; also the name of a Bengalese prophet born in 1485 A.D. who emphasized the path of divine love for the realization of God; he is also known as Gauranga or Gaura.

Chit: Consciousness.

Darśanas: The six systems of orthodox Hindu philosophy.

Dharma: (in Buddhism) Law of Life.

Durgā: A name of the Divine Mother.

Gayā: A sacred place in nothern India.

Gopāla: The baby Kṛṣṇa.

Govinda: A name of Sri Kṛṣṇa.

Guna: According to the Sāṅkhya philosophy Prakriti (nature), in contrast with Purusa (soul), consists of three gunas (qualities or strands) known as sattva, rajas, and tamas. Tamas stands for inertia or dullness, rajas for activity or restlessness, and sattva for balance or wisdom.

Hari: A name of God Vishnu, the Ideal Deity of the Vaishnavas.

Hathayoga: A school of yoga that aims chiefly at physical health and well-being.

Indra: The Hindu mythological king of gods.
Ishta-Devata: The Chosen Ideal or Ideal Deity of the devotee.
Iśvara: The personal God.

Jīva: The embodied soul; an ordinary man.
Jnāna: Knowledge of God arrived at through reasoning and discrimination.

Kāla: A name of Śiva; black; death; time.
Kāli: A name of the Divine Mother.
Karmayoga: Union with God through action; the path by which the aspirant seeks to realize God through work without attachment.
Karma: Action in general; duty; ritualistic worship.
Kṛṣṇa: God as Lord; the Avātar of the Bhagavad Gītā; one of the Ideal Deities of the Vaishnavas.
Kundalini: Serpent power; it is the spiritual energy that lies dormant in all individuals (it is an involved concept-process fully explained in Tāntrik teachings).

Līlā: The divine play; the relative; the creation as explained by the Vaishnavas as the Līlā of God, a concept that introduces elements of freedom and spontaneity into the Universe.

Mahābhārata: A great Hindu epic.
Mahādeva: The Great God; a name of Śiva.
Māyā: Ignorance obscuring the vision of God; the Cosmic illusion on account of which the One appears as many, the Absolute as the Relative; it denotes attachment.
Mukti: Liberation from the bondage of the world.

Nārada: A great sage and lover of God.
Nārāyana: The name of Vishnu.
Nārāyani: The consort of Nārāyana; the name of the Divine Mother.
Nirvāna: Final absorption in Brahman, or the All-pervading Reality, by the annihilation of the individual ego.
Nyāya: Indian logic; one of the six systems of orthodox Hindu philosophy.

Prakriti: Primordial nature, which, in association with Puruṣa, creates the universe (used appreciably in the formulations of the Sāṅkhya philosophy).
Prāna: The vital breath that sustains life in the physical body.
Prānāyāma: Control of breath; one of the disciplines of yoga.
Puruṣa: According to Sāṅkhya denotes the eternal conscious (Eastern) principle; the universe evolves from the union of Prakriti and Puruṣa.

Rādhā: Sri Kṛṣṇa's most intimate companion among the gopis of Vrindāvan.
Raghuvir: A name of Rāma; the family Deity of Ramakrishna.
Rāma: The hero of the Rāmāyāna regarded as a Divine Incarnation.
Rāmāyana: A well known Hindu epic.
Rāmprasad: The Bengali mystic and writer of songs to the Divine Mother.
Rishis: Seers, inspired sages or religious poets.

Sādhaka: An aspirant devoted to the practice of spiritual discipline.
Sadhana: Spiritual discipline.
Samadhi: Ecstasy, trance, communion with God.
Sāṅkhya: One of the six orthodox Hindu systems of philosophy.
Sannyāsi: A Hindu monk.
Siddha: (literally perfect or boiled) applies both to perfected beings and to boiled things.

Siddhi: Perfection in spiritual life (as used in this study).
Sīta: The wife of Śiva.
Śiva: The destroyer God; the third Person of the Hindu Trinity; also God the Lord.
Sri: Used as a prefix to the name of a Hindu man, corresponding to Mr.
Sumeru: The sacred mount Meru of Hindu mythology.

Tantra: A system of religious philosophy in which the Divine Mother, or Power is the Ultimate Reality; also the scripture of this system.
Tāntrik: A follower of Tantra or pertaining to Tantra.

Upadesa: Instruction, pertaining particularly to religious-spiritual matters.
Upaniṣads: The well known scriptures of the Hindus.
Upāsāna: Worship.

Vaishnava: Follower of Vishnu.
Vedanta: One of the six orthodox systems of Hindu philosophy.
Vishnu: The preserver God; the second person in the Hindu Trinity; the personal God of the Vaishnavas.
Vrindāvan: A town associated with Sri Kṛṣṇa's childhood.

Yoga: Union of the individual soul and the Universal Soul; also the method by which to realize this union.
Yogi: One who practices yoga.
Yogini: Woman Yogi.

[1] C.G. Jung, *Two Essays on Analytical Psychology*, Vol. 7 of *The Collected Works* (London: Routledge & Kegan Paul, 1953); see also C.G. Jung, *Psychological Types*, Vol. 6, Part II of *The Collected Works* (New York: Pantheon Books).

[2] Swami Nikhilananda, *The Gospel of Ramakrishna* (Madras: Sri Ramakrishna Math, 1964 ed.), pp. 1029-1056; see also Ernest Wood, *Yoga Dictionary* (New York: Philosophical Library, 1956), 178 pp.; and Ernest Wood, *Vedanta Dictionary* (New York: Philosophical Library, 1964), 225 pp.

BIBLIOGRAPHY

Books

Adler, G. *Studies In Analytical Psychology.* New York: G. P. Putnam's Sons, 1967. 250 pp.

_____. *Success and Failure in Analysis.* New York: G. P. Putnam's Sons, 1974. 231 pp.

Agehanada, B. *The Tantrik Tradition.* London: Rider & Co., 1965. 350 pp.

Ames, Van Meter. *Zen & American Thought.* Honolulu: University of Hawaii Press, 1962. 293 pp.

Avalon, Arthur. (Sir John Woodroffe). *Principles of Tantra.* Madras: Ganesh & Co., Provate Ltd., 1960. 787 pp.

Badarayana. *The Brahma Sutra.* Trans., S. Radhakrishnan. London: George Allen & Unwin Ltd., 1960. 606 pp.

Benoit, Hubert. *Let Go.* London: George Allen & Unwin Ltd., 1962. 277 pp.

Bertine, Eleanor. *Human Relationships.* New York: Longman's, 1958 (reprinted 1963). 237 pp.

_____. *Jung's Contributions to Our Time.* New York: G. P. Putnam's Sons, 1967. 269 pp.

_____. *Jung's Contributions to Our Time. The Collected Papers of Eleanor Bertine.* E. C. Rorhback (ed.) New York: G.P. Putnam's Sons, 1967. 271 pp.

Blofeld, J. *The Zen Teaching of Hui Hai.* London: Rider & Co., 1962. 160 pp.

_____. *The Tantric Mysticism of Tibet.* New York: E. P. Dutton & Co., 1970. 257 pp.

Blyth, R. H. *Zen and Zen Classics.* Tokyo: The Hokuseido Press, 1960.

Brent, P. *Godmen of India.* Chicago: Quadrangle Books, 1972. 346 pp.

Campbell, J. *The Hero With a Thousand Faces.* New York: Pantheon Books, 1949. 416 pp.

Chang, C. *Teaching of Tibetan Yoga.* New York: University Books, 1963. 128 pp.

Chapman, Rick. *How to Choose a Guru.* New York: Harper, 1973. 285 pp.

Chatterjee, S. & D. Datta. *An Introduction to Indian Philosophy.* Calcutta: University of Calcutta Press, 1960. 437 pp.

Chatterji, H. *The Bhagavad Gītā.* New York: The Julian Press, 1960. 283 pp.

Chaudhuri, H. *Integral Yoga.* London: George Allen & Unwin Ltd., 1965. 160 pp.

_____, and F. Spiegelberg, (eds.). *The Integral Philosophy of Sri Aurobindo, A Commemorative Symposium.* London: George Allen & Unwin Ltd., 1960. 350 pp.

Conze, E. *Buddhism, Its Essence and Development.* Oxford: Cassirer Publishers, 1953. 212 pp.

115

————, et al. *Buddhist Texts Through the Ages*. New York: Philosophical Library, 1954. 322 pp.

Coomaraswami, A. K. *Hinduism and Buddhism*. New York: Philosophical Library, n.d. 86 pp.

————. *Buddha and the Gospel of Buddhism*. Bombay, Asia Publishing House, 1958. 370 pp.

David-Neel, A. *Initiations and Initiates in Tibet*. London: Rider & Co., 1931. 224 pp.

Das, S. C. *Contributions on the Religion and History of Tibet*. New Delhi: Manjusri Publishing House, 1970. 210 pp.

Dasgupta, S. *Introduction to Tāntrik Buddhism*. Calcutta: University of Calcutta Press, 1958. 211 pp.

Durant, W. *The Story of Civilization*. Vol. 1, *Our Oriental Heritage*. New York: Simon & Schuster, 1954. pp. 389-1049.

Dry, A. *The Psychology of Jung: A Critical Interpretation*. London: Methuen & Co., Ltd., 1961. 329 pp.

Edinger, E. *Ego & Archetype*. New York: Putnam's Sons, 1972. 304 pp.

Eliade, M. *Birth and Rebirth: The Religious Meaning of Initiation in Human Culture*. New York: Harper & Co., 1958. 175 pp.

————. *Patterns of Comparative Religion*. Cleveland: The World Publishing Co., 1963. 484 pp.

————. *Yoga: Immortality and Freedom*. New York: Pantheon Books, 1958. 528 pp.

Evans-Wentz, W. Y. *The Tibetan Book of the Great Liberation*. London: Oxford University Press, 1960. 249 pp.

————. *Tibetan Yoga and Secret Doctrines*. London: Oxford University Press, 1958. 389 pp.

————. (ed.) *Tibet's Great Yogi Milarepa*. London: Oxford University Press, 1951. 3rd impression, 1963. 315 pp.

Fingarette, H. *The Self in Transformation: Psychoanalysis, Philosophy and the Life of the Spirit*. New York: Basic Books, 1963. 356 pp.

Fordham, M. (ed.) *Contact With Jung: Essays on the Influence of his Work and Personality*. London: Tavistock Publishing Co., 1963. 245 pp.

————. *The Objective Psyche*. London: Routledge, 1958. 214 pp.

————. *New Developments in Analytical Psychology*. London: Routledge and Kegan Paul, 1957. 214 pp.

Fordham, F. *Introduction to Jung's Psychology*. London: Penguin Books, 1953. 128 pp.

Fromm, Erich. *The Forgotten Language: An Introduction to the Understanding of Dreams, Fairy Tales and Myths*. New York: Rinehart, 1951. 263 pp.

————, et al. *Zen Buddhism and Psychoanalysis*. New York: Harper, 1960. 180 pp.

Garrison, O. V. *Tantrism: The Yoga of Sex*. New York: Julian Press, 1964. 252 pp.

Ghose (Sri Aurobindo). *Essays on the Gītā*. Calcutta: Arya Publishing House, 5th ed., 1949. 322 pp.

————. *Sri Aurobindo On the Veda*. Pondicherry: Sri Aurobindo Ashram, 1956. 671 pp.

————. *The Synthesis of Yoga*. New York: Sri Aurobindo Library, Inc., 1950. 303 pp.

————. *On Yoga II - Tome One*. Pondicherry: Sri Aurobindo Ashram, 1958. 843 pp.

Govinda, A. *The Psychological Attitude of Early Buddhist Philosophy*. London: Rider & Co., 1961. 192 pp.

Guenther, H. V. *The Life and Teachings of Naropa*. Oxford: Clarendon Press, 1963. 292 pp.

————. *Treasures on the Tibetan Middle Way*. Berkeley: Shambala Publishing Ltd., 1969. 148pp.

Hall, C., and Lindsey, C. *Theories of Personality.* New York: Willey & Co., 1957. 572 pp.

Hannah, B. *Striving Toward Wholeness.* New York: G. P. Putnam's Sons, 1971. 316 pp.

Harding, Esther. *Psychic Energy: Its Source and Goal.* New York: Pantheon Books, 1948. 497 pp.

_____. *Journey Into Self.* New York: Longmans, Green & Co., 1956. 301 pp.

_____. *The Parental Image: Its Image and Reconstruction. A Study in Analytical Psychology.* New York: G. P. Putnam's Sons, 1965. 238 pp.

_____. *The Way of All Women: A Psychological Interpretation.* London: Longmans & Co., 1933. 335 pp.

Harper, M. H. *Gurus, Swamis, and Avataras.* Philadelphia: The Westminster Press, 1972.

Herrigel, E. *The Method of Zen.* New York: Pantheon Books, 1960. 124 pp.

_____. *Zen In the Art of Archery.* New York: Pantheon Books, 1953. 109 pp.

Humphreys, C. *Zen A Way of Life.* New York: Emerson Books, 1965. 199 pp.

James, William. *The Varieties of Religious Experience.* New York: Mentor Books of the New American Library of World Literature, Inc., 1958. 406 pp.

Isherwood, Christopher. *Ramakrishna and His Disciples.* New York: Simon & Schuster, 1965. 365 pp.

Jung, Carl G. *The Collected Works.* Bollingen Series No. XX. New York: Pantheon Books.

Psychiatric Studies. Vol. 1, 1957.
The Psychogenesis of Mental Disease. Vol. 3, 1960.
Freud and Psychoanalysis. Vol. 4, 1961.
Symbols of Transformation. Vol. 5, 1956.
Psychological Types. Vol. 6, 1964. Earlier Printing, 1923.
Two Essays in Analytical Psychology. Vol. 7, 1953.
The Structure and Dynamics of the Psyche. Vol. 8, 1960.
The Archetypes of the Collective Unconscious. Vol. 9, Part I, 1959.
Aion: Researches into the Phenomenology of the Psyche. Vol. 9, Part II, 1959.
Civilization in Transition. Vol. 10, 1964.
Psychology and Religion: West and East. Vol. 11, 1958.
Psychology and Alchemy. Vol. 12, 1953.
Mysterium Coniunctionis. Vol. 14, 1963.
The Spirit in Man, Art and Literature. Vol. 15, 1954.
The Practice of Psychotherapy. Vol. 16, 1954.
The Development of Personality. Vol. 17, 1954 ed. 2nd printing with corrections, 1964.

_____. *Memories, Dreams, Reflections.* New York: Pantheon Books, 1962. 298 pp.

_____. *Psychological Reflections: A Jung Anthology.* New York: Pantheon Books, 1953. 342 pp.

_____, and Kerenyi, C. *Essays On a Science of Mythology.* New York: Bollingen Foundation by Pantheon Books, Inc., 1949. 289 pp.

Legge, James. *The Texts of Taoism.* New York: Julian Press, 1959. 790 pp.

Linsen, Robert. *Living Zen.* London: George Allen & Unwin, Ltd., 1958. 368 pp.

Maharshi, Ramana. *Golden Jubilee Souvenir.* Tiruvannamalai, So. India: Sri Ramanashrama, 1949. 376 pp.

_____. *Talks With Sri Ramana Maharshi.* Tiruvannamalai, So. India: Sri Ramanashrama. Vol. I, II, & III, 1955.

Muller, Max. *Ramakrishna His Life and Sayings.* Mayamati Almora, Himalayas: Advaita Ashrama, 1951. 200 pp.

Marshall, Anne. *Hunting the Guru in India.* London: Victor Collanz Ltd., 1963. 208 pp.

Mishra, H.S. *The Textbook of Yoga Psychology.* New York: The Julian Press, Inc. 1963. 402 pp.

Nikhilananda, Swami. *Samkaracarya Self-Knowledge.* New York: Ramakrishna-Vivekananda Center, 1946. 228 pp.

———. *The Bhagavad Gītā.* New York: Ramakrishna-Vivekananda Center, 1944. 386 pp.

——— (trans.). *The Gospel of Sri Ramakrishna.* New York: Ramakrishna-Vivekananda Center, 1942. 1063 pp.

Neumann, Erich. *The Origins and History of Consciousness.* New York: Bollingen Foundation by Pantheon Books, Inc., 1953, 493 pp.

Ogata, Sohaku. *Zen for the West.* London, Rider & Co., 1959, 182 pp.

Osborne, Arthur. *Ramana Maharshi and the Path of Self-Knowledge.* London: Rider & Co., 1957. 207 pp.

Powell, Robert. *Zen and Reality.* New York: Taplinger Co., 1961. 141 pp.

Progoff, Ira. *Depth Psychology and Modern Man.* New York: The Julian Press, 1959.

———. *The Symbolic and the Real.* New York: The Julian Press, 1963. 234 pp.

———. *The Death and Rebirth of Psychology:* An Interpretive Evaluation of Freud, Adler, Jung and Rank and the Impact of Their Culminating Insights on Modern Man. New York: Julian Press, 1956. 274 pp.

Radhakrishnan, S. (ed. and trans.). *The Principal Upaniṣads.* London: George Allen & Unwin Ltd., 1953. 958 pp.

———. *Indian Philosophy.* Vol. I and II. London: George Allen & Unwin Ltd., 1929.

Ramana, Bhagavan (ed. by A. Osborne). *The Collected Works of Ramana Maharshi.* London: Rider & Co., 1959. 192 pp.

Reps, Paul. *Zen Flesh Zen Bones.* Tokyo: Charles E. Tuttle Co., 1957. 211 pp.

Rogers, Carl H. *On Becoming a Person.* Boston: Houghton Mifflin Co., 1961. 420 pp.

Ross, N. W. *The World of Zen.* New York: Random House, 1960. 362 pp.

Sanford, J. *Dreams; God's Forgotten Language.* Philadelphia: Lippincott, 1968. 223 pp.

Saradananda, Swami. *Sri Ramakrishna the Great Master.* Madras: Sri Ramakrishna Math. 1952. 950 pp.

Sharma, C. *Indian Philosophy: A Critical Survey.* London: Rider & Co., 1960. U.S. ed. by Barnes & Noble, Inc., 1962. 405 pp.

Singer, J. *Boundaries of the Soul: The Practice of Jung's Psychology.* Garden City, New York: Doubleday, 1972. 420 pp.

Smart, N. *The Yogi and the Devotee.* London: George Allen & Unwin Ltd., 1968. 174 pp.

Snellgrove, D.L. *Buddhist Himalaya.* Oxford: Bruno Cassirer Ltd., 1957. 324 pp.

Speigelberg, Frederic. *Living Religions of the World.* Englewood Cliffs: Prentice Hall, Inc., 1956. 511 pp.

Suzuki, D. T. *Essays in Zen Buddhism.* London: Rider & Co., 1951 and later editions. Series 1, 2, 3, & 4.

———. *Mahāyāna Buddhism.* New York: The MacMillan Co., 1959. 147 pp.

———. *Zen and Japanese Buddhism.* Tokyo: Japan Travel Bureau, 1961. 150 pp.

———. *Zen and Japanese Culture.* New York: Pantheon Books, 1959. 478 pp.

———. *Laṅkāvatāra Sūtra.* London: Routledge & Kegan Paul Ltd., 1932. 300 pp.

———. *Manual of Zen Buddhism.* London: Rider & Co., 1950. 192 pp.

———. *Outlines of Mahayana Buddhism.* New York: Schocken Books, 1963, 383 pp.

Tucci, Giuseppe. *The Theory and Practice of the Mandala.* London: Rider & Co., 1961. 147 pp.

Venkataranan, T. N. (ed.). *Day by Day With Bhagavan.* Tiruvannamalai: Sri Ramanashramam, 1957. Vol. I & II.

Vilayat, Pir. *Toward the One.* New York: Harper & Row Publishers, Inc., 1974. 678 pp.

Watts, Alan W. *Psychotherapy East and West.* New York: Pantheon Books, 1961. 204 pp.

—————. *The Spirit of Zen.* New York: Grove Press, Inc., 1960 ed. 128 pp.

—————. *This Is It.* New York: Pantheon Books, 1960. 158 pp.

Weaver, Rix. *The Old Wise Woman.* New York: G. P. Putnam's Sons, 1973. 174 pp.

Wheelwright, J. (ed.). *The Analytic Process.* New York: C. G. Jung Foundation for Analytical Psychology by G. P. Putnam's Sons, 1971. 316 pp.

Wickes, Frances. *The Inner World of Man.* New York: Ungar, 1943. 313 pp.

—————. *The Inner World of Choice.* New York: Harper, 1963. 318 pp.

—————. *The Inner World of Childhood.* New York: Appelton Century, 1965 revised ed. 342 pp.

Wood, Ernest. *Yoga Dictionary.* New York: Philosophical Library, 1956. 178 pp.

—————. *Vedanta Dictionary.* New York: Philosophical Library, 1964. 225 pp.

Woodroffe, Sir John. *Tantraraja Tantra.* Madras: Ganesh, 1954. 117 pp.

Zimmer, Heinrich. *Myths and Symbols In Indian Art and Civilization.* New York: Harper Torchbook, ed., 1962. 248 pp.

Publications of Learned Societies

Adler, G. "Current Trends In Analytical Psychology," *Proceedings of the First International Congress for Analytical Psychology.* London: Travistock Publications. 1961.

—————. "On the Archetype Content of Transference," *Report of the International Congress of Psychotherapy.* New York: 1955.

Guggenbuhl-Craig (ed.). "The Archetype," *Proceedings of the Second International Congress for Analytical Psychology.* Zurich, 1962. Basel/New York: S. Karger, 1964. 234 pp.

Henderson, J. L. "Resolution of the Transference in the Light of C. G. Jung's Psychology," *Report of the International Congress of Psychotherapy.* New York, 1955. pp. 75 ff.

Moody, R. "The Relation of Personal and Transpersonal Elements in the Transference." *Report of the International Congress of Psychotherapy.* New York, 1955. pp. 531 ff.

Plaut, A. "Research into Transference Phenomena," *Report of the International Congress of Psychotherapy.* New York, 1955.

Stein, L. "The Terminology of the Transference." *Report of the International Congress of Psychotherapy.* New York, 1955.

Periodicals

Adler, G. "Ego Integration Patterns of Coniunctio," *Journal of Analytical Psychology,* IV, No. 2, (July, 1959), 153.

Edinger, F.P. "The Ego Self Paradox," *Journal of Analytical Psychology,* V, No. 1, (January, 1960), 3.

Fordham, M. "Reflections on Image and Symbol," *Journal of Analytical Psychology,* II, No. 1, (January, 1957), 85.

—————. "The Evolution of Jung's Researches," *British Journal of Medical Psychology,* XXIX, 3. (1956).

—————. "Symposium on Training," *Journal of Analytical Psychology,* III, No. 2, (July, 1961), 95.

Gordon, R. "The Concept of Projective Identification: An Evaluation," *Journal of Analytical Psychology,* X, No. 2 (July, 1965), 127.

Kraemer, W. P. "The Dangers of Unrecognized Counter-transference," *Journal of Analytical Psychology*, III, No. 2.

Meier, C. A. "Projection Transference and the Subject-Object Relation in Psychology," *Journal of Analytical Psychology*, IV, No. 1, (January, 1959), 21.

Moody, R. "On the Function of the Counter-Transference," *Journal of Analytical Psychology*, I, No. 1, (October, 1949).

Paulsen, L. "Transference and Projection," *Journal of Analytical Psychology*, I, No. 1, (October, 1955), 203.

Plaut, A. "The Transference in Analytical Psychology," *British Journal of Medical Psychology*, XXIX, Part 1, (1956) 15 ff.

Dictionaries and Encyclopedias

Deutsch, A. and H. Fishman (eds.). *The Encyclopedia of Mental Health*, Six vols. New York: Watts, Inc., 1963.

Gray, L. H. (eds.). *The Mythology of All Races*. Vol. 13. New York: Cooper Square Publishing, Inc., 1964 ed.

Grinstein, A. *The Index of Psychoanalytic Writings*. Nine vols. New York: International Universities Press, Inc., 1956-1966.

Hastings, James (ed.). *The Encyclopedia of Religion and Ethics*. Twelve Vols. and index. New York: Charles Scribner's Sons, 1955.

Unpublished Material

Marsh, R. "A Comparative Analysis of the Concept of Individuality in the Thought of C. G. Jung and Sri Aurobindo." Unpublished Doctor's dissertation, University of Pacific through the American Academy of Asian Studies, 1959.